What to Do at 80

What to Do at 80

Ten-year plans

Arthur J. Paone

ISBN 978-1-7335191-0-6 (Digital)
ISBN 978-1-7335191-1-3 (Print)
Library of Congress Control Number: 2018914857

Table of Contents

Introduction

You may be smiling at the apparent incongruity of ten-year plans for people turning eighty, already a nice hefty age. There is, of course, good reason for your skepticism. Our National Center for Health Statistics has produced a Life Expectancy Chart that says that *on average*, a newborn in the US will not even reach the grand old age of eighty.

But I am not writing about newly born Americans, but about those of us who have already endured or escaped the many perils of life and have reached the ripe age of eighty. The fact is that if you make it to eighty, according to the same NCHS Chart, the odds are in your favor that you have another eight to ten years. Hence, *What to Do at Eighty*.

Table A. Expectation of life, by age, race, Hispanic origin, race for the non-Hispanic population, and sex: United States, 2014

Age (years)	All races and origins			White			Black			Hispanic[1]			Non-Hispanic white[1]			Non-Hispanic black[1]		
	Total	Male	Female	Total	Male	Female	Total	Male	Female	Total	Male	Female	Total	Male	Female	Total	Male	Female
0	78.9	76.5	81.3	79.1	76.7	81.4	75.6	72.5	78.5	82.1	79.4	84.5	78.8	76.5	81.2	75.3	72.2	78.2
1	78.3	76.0	80.7	78.5	76.1	80.8	75.5	72.4	78.3	81.5	78.8	83.8	78.2	75.9	80.6	75.1	72.0	78.0
5	74.4	72.0	76.8	74.5	72.2	76.8	71.6	68.5	74.4	77.5	74.9	79.9	74.3	72.0	76.6	71.3	68.2	74.1
10	69.5	67.1	71.8	69.6	67.3	71.9	66.7	63.6	69.4	72.6	69.9	74.9	69.3	67.0	71.6	66.3	63.2	69.1
15	64.5	62.1	66.8	64.6	62.3	66.9	61.7	58.6	64.5	67.6	65.0	70.0	64.4	62.1	66.7	61.4	58.3	64.2
20	59.7	57.3	61.9	59.8	57.5	62.0	56.9	53.9	59.6	62.7	60.1	65.0	59.5	57.3	61.8	56.6	53.6	59.3
25	54.9	52.7	57.0	55.0	52.6	57.1	52.2	49.3	54.7	57.9	55.4	60.2	54.8	52.6	56.9	51.9	49.0	54.5
30	50.2	48.0	52.2	50.2	48.1	52.3	47.5	44.8	49.9	53.1	50.7	55.3	50.0	47.9	52.1	47.3	44.5	49.7
35	45.4	43.4	47.4	45.5	43.5	47.5	42.9	40.3	45.2	48.3	46.9	50.4	45.3	43.3	47.3	42.6	40.0	44.9
40	40.7	38.8	42.6	40.8	38.9	42.7	38.3	35.8	40.5	43.8	41.2	45.5	40.7	38.7	42.5	38.1	35.8	40.3
45	36.1	34.2	38.0	36.2	34.3	38.0	33.9	31.4	36.0	38.9	36.6	40.7	36.1	34.2	37.9	33.6	31.2	35.7
50	31.7	29.8	33.4	31.7	29.9	33.4	29.5	27.2	31.5	34.3	32.1	36.1	31.6	29.8	33.3	29.3	27.0	31.3
55	27.4	25.6	29.0	27.4	25.7	29.0	25.5	23.2	27.4	29.8	27.7	31.5	27.3	25.7	28.9	25.3	23.0	27.2
60	23.3	21.7	24.7	23.3	21.8	24.7	21.7	19.6	23.4	25.5	23.6	27.0	23.3	21.7	24.7	21.6	19.4	23.3
65	19.4	18.0	20.6	19.4	18.0	20.6	18.2	16.4	18.7	21.5	19.7	22.8	19.3	18.0	20.5	18.1	16.3	19.5
70	15.7	14.5	16.7	15.7	14.5	16.6	14.9	13.3	16.1	17.6	16.0	18.7	15.6	14.4	16.6	14.8	13.2	16.0
75	12.3	11.2	13.1	12.2	11.2	13.0	11.9	10.6	12.8	13.9	12.6	14.8	12.2	11.2	13.0	11.8	10.5	12.7
80	9.2	8.4	9.8	9.2	8.3	9.7	9.2	8.2	9.8	10.6	9.5	11.2	9.1	8.3	9.7	9.2	8.1	9.8
85	6.7	6.0	7.1	6.5	5.9	7.0	6.9	6.1	7.3	7.8	6.9	8.2	6.6	5.9	7.0	6.9	6.1	7.3
90	4.6	4.1	4.9	4.6	4.1	4.8	5.1	4.5	5.4	5.5	4.8	5.7	4.6	4.1	4.8	5.1	4.5	5.4
95	3.2	2.9	3.4	3.2	2.8	3.3	3.8	3.3	3.9	3.8	3.3	3.9	3.2	2.8	3.3	3.8	3.4	3.9
100	2.3	2.1	2.3	2.2	2.0	2.3	2.8	2.5	2.9	2.7	2.4	2.7	2.2	2.0	2.3	2.9	2.6	2.9

[1]Life tables by Hispanic origin are based on death rates that have been adjusted for race and ethnicity misclassification on death certificates. Updated classification ratios were applied; see Technical Notes.
SOURCE: NCHS, National Vital Statistics System, Mortality.

I entered my eighth decade on August 8, 2018, my seventy-ninth birthday, a couple of months before I started this book. That was the inevitable consequence of the fact that I was born on August 8, 1939.

My brother Big Jimmy was also born on August 8. We were both Leos and shared the same birthday all our lives. He did so until last December, when he died, in a nursing home, at eighty-six. He was eighty-six when he died because he was born in 1931. Since I am the only one of our siblings left with any capacity to do such things, I had him cremated and then set up a little goodbye ceremony to pay Jimmy our respects.

As it happened, I found myself in a hospital when the memorial took place. But more on that in a little bit.

I carried Jimmy's remains in my car trunk till I got a chance to go to the cemetery and arrange his burial. The idiots there required, aside from $1,700, a letter from his parish priest that he was a parishioner in good standing before they would allow him to be buried among the other good Christians in sacred grounds. Poor guy was well beyond reason by the time he left us, but he qualified otherwise, and we got him buried in the same grave with our parents and two sisters. Seemed the right thing to do.

So, at seventy-nine now, I am thinking about eighty and beyond. I barely made it to this point. In December of last year, just before Jimmy died, I was hit right in the face with a case of shingles. Painful and awful looking. But it did not develop into its worst debilitating type, and it mostly passed in a couple of weeks. In the middle of this, I had to go up to Brooklyn and see a funeral director about Jimmy. The guy showed no reaction to my still-bloodied nose and puffy face.

Barely thereafter, on January 1 of this year, 2018, I found myself in agony, this time with awful pains in my stomach. My wife and I took off in the middle of the night to the local emergency room. I got operated on for a busted appendix. Just made it. Great people there—the doctors and nurses. But here I am, and I am making plans for my eighties. Seems I am being especially brash in assuming that I will even make it to eighty, in light of my recent close call. But let's go anyway. Hell, what else can one do? Couldn't function otherwise.

I am excited by the idea of "my eighties." It's something new for me that I had never thought of before. I feel that the eighties is a significant and special category. Also, it seems logical that I should plan for my eighties and that my eighties should have a plan to it.

As I started to think more about this and talked to my friends—yes, I do have some friends, primarily fellow dog owners who walk at a beach on the Jersey Shore each day, then have some coffee and share the news and our stories—I found that the subject deserved to be a "Project."

Since any project would require a lot of thinking and working, I thought it would be a shame to keep what would surely be a great body of thinking and working just to myself or my small circle of friends. I figured there must be tons of people who will be entering their eighties and could benefit from my efforts. I could even monetize my work to supplement what we have to live on. Hence, this book is perhaps my last chance (not counting lottery tickets) to strike it rich and achieve Fame and Fortune.

Now, you cannot have one plan "that fits all," or, as one enterprising Vietnamese or Cambodian factory wryly labels its hats, "that fits most." Both the rich and the poor can reach their eighties. So do the smart and the dumb. Men and women. Techs and nontechs. People with families and those alone. The strong and the weak. Optimists and pessimists. God-fearing people and nonbelievers. Those with friends and the friendless. The healthy and the sickly.

You get my point. There has to be a bunch of plans so that a reader might find one that he or she both likes and feels able to follow. A reader could also jump from one Plan to another. There are no rules. Whatever works for you.

At the same time, all the plans will have to take "diminishment" into consideration. Let's just admit up front that we are not what we used to be. Of course, there may be rare exceptions to this rule, but I am not dealing with the one-offs here—just us folks.

Diminished energy. Diminished hope. Diminished memory. Diminished reflexes. Diminished hearing. Diminished sight. Diminished movement—both in brain and body. Diminished sex drive or whatever. And all the other diminishments of life. It is just that way, and I will factor that into each Plan. No pie-in-the sky stuff. We are not going to have ten-year plans for marathoners or brain surgeons or nuclear scientists or app and game developers. Again, just us folks.

Finally, each Plan will be just a framework. If you see something you like, play with it till it suits you and then go with it. The details will fall into place as you go along. So let's get to it.

The Doing Nothing Plan

Under this Plan, you let each day take care of itself.

This is a plan that works best for those who still have some mental flexibility. Not everyone can face an empty slate in the morning. It is not for the dull of mind or the stupid among us. These latter can't be presented with too much freedom, or they will end up actually doing nothing, staring into space and vegetating.

I have been in this Plan myself for some time already. When people ask me what I do, I say "Nothing." They always find that amusing (my intention), though of course they do not understand what I really mean.

A Doing Nothing Plan does not mean doing nothing, but, rather, it means ordinarily not making any plans for what you will be doing that day. You just take it as it comes. Let the day take you where it leads.

Under a Doing Nothing Plan, you wake up in the morning with no idea what your day will be like.

You start with a conversation with yourself. Something like: "How do I feel?" "What do I feel up to today?" "I wonder what is happening at the Dunkin' Donuts?" "Maybe I'll walk to the park and see who is around."

Some activity forces itself on you. For instance, if you have a dog or a number of dogs, you have to take them out. That starts the day rolling. Then you need to shower and eat. Any promises left over from yesterday have to be fulfilled. Did you promise to call someone? Is there something in the yard or garden that needs attention? Is the floor clean, or does it need some sweeping or mopping? Have I cleaned the sheets recently? What was that I saw yesterday down the block? Were they making changes on that old house? Let's go see.

You go down the block and watch the people working on the house for a while. Maybe others are also watching, and you chat with them. You compare observations and maybe continue the conversation over coffee. Or you might not see anything interesting and just go back home.

Back home, the screen door gets stuck. You spend the rest of the day fixing it. No need to rush, as you have the rest of your life to fix it.

On other days there may be interventions from outside. Someone comes to visit. You need to prepare, so you go out and buy something. You spend some time with them, and maybe they have some idea of something else to do. You may or may not join them. The day runs its course.

The Making Friends Plan

We each have a spark in us, and friends are the best way to keep that spark going.

We tell them our stories and hear theirs. We share what we are going to do today and what we did yesterday. Together we could figure the world out.

"What's happening?"

"How you doing?"

Time has taken many people we have known to the next world. That is why we need to make extra efforts to fill that void.

Here is the secret to accumulating as many or as few friends as you can take—but friends you must have. The secret is as follows:

Each day, visit the same place at the same time,
and stay for a while.

That's it.

You will sometimes see the same faces. After a while you get a nodding acquaintance. Then, sometime later, you may pass a word or two. From that word or two, you will know—this could, or could not, be a friend.

Keep doing the same thing. The few words with some might expand to little conversations—about the weather, the place you both are sitting, the news, perhaps. After a while, you may be looking forward to seeing that person. Before long, you are routinely sharing stories, news of the day—you have a new friend.

Go to places you like. The people you find there will have at least that in common—they like it too. That is a beginning to build a friendship on.

It could be a library, a Dunkin' Donuts, a good spot in the park or on the boardwalk, the gym, whatever.

Let's just do it.

As it happened in my life, I met my latest gang of friends down here in Belmar when I started walking Buddy on the beach each day. First it was Nancy, and she introduced me to Mary, who would have Nancy and me over for coffee at her beautiful house after our walk. Over time, others joined Nancy and Mary, and we would have quite a group gathering at Mary's after our walk. Sometimes just a couple of people with their dogs; other times eight to twelve people. It changed often. Beautiful way to start the day. Mary and a few of her friends even got the town to officially approve an out-of-the-way spot on the beach designated as a dog park for certain hours of the day.

Taking Care of Grandchildren Plan

This Plan requires that you actually *have* grandchildren. It will not do for you to volunteer to take care of someone else's grandchildren. As sad as it may seem to you, such requests may throw suspicions of perversion upon you. Just put this into the category of "No good deed goes unpunished," and move on.

Even for those with grandchildren, this Plan is an acquired taste and is suitable only for those who have retained some patience and energy.

The regulations for this program will limit the time involved—no more than two hours on any day and no more than twice a week. We don't want the program to backfire. That is the risk in all these Plans—the risk of backfire.

We want to be nice, help the kids, and have fun at the same time. But if you have too much of the little fuckers, you may do or say things that others may consider inappropriate—or, God forbid, you may even become violent. So the major point in the Plan involving grandchildren is strict limitation of time and exposure.

Writing "Letters to the Editor" Plan

There are those among us eighty-pluses who feel the need to complain about everything. Then there are those of us who used to grumble about something now and then but find themselves crabbing about something or other a lot more now. This Plan is for those who have filled the air with gripes all their lives as well as those who are just now tasting the joys of grousing.

For the cantankerous, there is a whole new world out there. You used to be limited to complaining to those around you and writing a Letter to the Editor. Of course, the ignorant idiot at the receiving end of your carefully written missive would more than likely just throw it into the garbage.

But now, with the internet, you can get your diatribes out there, whether anybody likes it or not.

You can use one of the commercial platforms, such as Facebook or the like. Or you can easily set up one yourself. How to complain endlessly and get it out there in the universe—whether they like it or not.

Go to Google and put in "social media." Then take your pick of what groups you want to join—there is a group for everything and everybody. Find out who is compatible with you and go pester them. Or pick the ones who are not compatible and pester them.

You do not need worry about how to do these things. There are lots of sites where someone is eager to show you how to do it. Just check it out. You could get on dozens of sites and became a royal pain in the ass in no time. Just do it. There are few rules, so you can spill your spleen all over the place. Don't worry—you are not messing things up; it already is a mess. You can even find a place to complain that it is all a mess.

The Traveling Plan

Traveling and seeing the world may be the wish of many of us eighty-pluses. But wishing is not enough. Even more than our diminished energy and patience, there is the matter of money. This Plan is limited primarily to people with a decent modicum of energy and, more importantly, lots of money.

That is because when I say "travel," I do not mean getting to the mall or downtown. I mean far-away places. Local travel for us has become easier with mass transit, taxis, and the mushrooming likes of Uber and Lift. Incidentally, please don't fight the family about giving up the car keys. Do everybody a favor and put them out of your life before everybody starts talking about it. You will know when it is time; just be sensible and give them up instead of reducing yourself to constant bickering with your loved ones.

For a traveling eighty-plus, you must have only the deluxe, first class, luxury, premium, exclusive, and the like. And this costs money. Nothing less will give you the comfort and safety that is required for you.

It is not just that you can buy a ticket for a cheap bus trip and look out the window at the world. The seats will be too uncomfortable. You cannot even step high enough to get into most buses. The bus has no bathroom and does not stop often enough for you to go. The bus bounces and rattles your bones. The person sitting next to you for twenty-two hours stinks.

The same with driving. You just can't drive far enough to call it traveling. Fuhgeddaboudit.

Flying is OK, but the hassle of getting to the airport and the crush and lines and checkpoints will quickly wear you out.

If you have lots of money, however, these prohibitive obstacles disappear. You can and will travel only in luxury. A car driven by someone else takes you to the airport. Someone else carries your bags. The tickets and arrangements have been made by agents. You get to the head of the line as a Special First-Class person or with membership in some Exclusive Club. You have entre to all the best clubs at the airport, so you can use clean bathrooms and rest in comfort during any delays.

Of course, you must be able to travel first class and only on the airlines that have luxury first class.

You need space, service, and comfort.

Then it will be the same on the other side of wherever you are going, with the added expense of translators. Easy off the plane and easy into the new city. Someone who has been contacted by one of your Exclusive Clubs gets you through customs quickly. Someone carries your bags and takes you to the hotel. The hotel has to have easy-access ramps and a lot of hands-on service people to help you get around.

Money, Money, and Money will let you Travel, Travel, and Travel under this Plan.

Otherwise, fuhgeddaboudit.

The Walking Plan

Most of us can do this. You need no equipment, training, or preparation, and it can be combined with other Plans.

The key to a successful Walking Plan is that you walk every day. It could be on the same route or different routes.

People living near large parks, lakes, and beaches will find this easier, but even in a crowded city, walking has its virtues. There are people to see and events happening in real time. The problem with crowded city walking is the lights and the corners and maybe even the crowds.

You will be able to determine in short order whether a Walking Plan is for you. Try it for a few days, and then think about it.

Needless to say—but it will be said—you will need good shoes. You can't skimp on this. Good, solid walking shoes. But don't wear a pair of new shoes every day after you buy them. You need to break them in and get your feet used to them. Wear them every other day, then every third day, then lay off for a week, then every other day for a while, and then I think they will be fine.

At the first hint of discomfort, you will need to examine the shoes and your fit. Don't continue to walk if your feet hurt. They hurt for a reason. Find out yourself and correct the issue (socks too thick or thin, crease at top of shoe, etc.). You may need either a shoemaker or a podiatrist to help you on this. Don't skimp. You cannot have a ten-year Walking Plan if you cannot walk comfortably.

Remember to bring you phone with you, hopefully one that takes pictures and voice recordings. You may want to stop and take a picture of something that strikes you—not a car—or record some interesting thoughts that are inspired by some sight. Also, in some cases you may need the map/directions app on the phone to find your way there and back.

Most of my walking has been with my dogs and on the beach. There is an infinite variety of shy-wave-people sights along the beach.

Not Falling Plan-Whatever You Do

This should be Plan Number One or even a subpart of every other Plan. Falls must be avoided at all costs—as falls often are the beginning of the end. Stay on your feet or sit down—just don't fall down.

I will outline a program for a no-fall lifestyle. It will be robust and include activity—but no falls. The program will also detail architectural layouts, construction material, and physical things that will help prevent falls or, if one does fall, alleviate the damage, if any. Forget about those call pendants. What the hell are they good for if you have already fallen and broken your leg!

Visiting Museums and Attending Lectures Plan

This Plan is easier for someone living in a large city where you can open the newspaper in the morning and find ten or twenty interesting lectures or exhibits going on at any time. But a modified version can be utilized in smaller localities, or it can be combined with another Plan to make it in a full Plan.

In writing this, I recall that when I lived in New York City, I always wondered why there was such an abundance of older people in attendance at free, public lectures. That tells me that this is another natural Plan for us eighty-pluses.

I remember, in particular, a presentation in the NYC Public Library at Thirty-Fourth Street. It was by the son of Alger Hiss, who had been accused by Whitaker Chambers of being a Soviet spy and convicted of perjury before Congress. The younger Hiss laid out his arguments for why his father had not been a spy. Some of them were persuasive, but I wondered what he was trying to accomplish by this effort. Did he think the people listening to him could do something about his now-dead father's reputation? I thought, "What's the use of his convincing a bunch of old people? They can't do anything about it anymore."

But now I am reevaluating my observation of that day. Who cares what the person making the presentation wants to accomplish? We are there not for him or her, but for ourselves. We are there to be entertained in one form or another. Perhaps to listen. Perhaps to watch the crowd. Perhaps to find a warm or cool place to spend some time. Perhaps to have some of the refreshments they may serve.

Lectures at libraries are free. So are events at churches, various societies, and art galleries. But you begin to run into fees at museums. One wonders what it is with museums.

They exist, I suppose, for public education, but they keep people out by charging them. Don't these institutions get enough money from our taxpayer government grants and from the robber barons and big-time thieves and barely legal criminals who donate money to them, so they can get their tax breaks as well as see their silly names on walls, rooms, and buildings? I suppose the rich not only want to grind us down but at the same time want us to praise them for their generosity.

Whose names are we forced to look at when we visit these museums? Probably the same ones that students have to look at on their newly renamed buildings in honor of alumni who have dropped big bucks on their schools. They are the great US industrialists who are in a constant and frenzied search to the bottom, seeking out the poorest of the poor to produce their goods in China, then Cambodia, then Vietnam, then Bangladesh—anywhere in the world except in the United States, where they would have to pay living wages.

The very people who have impoverished so many cities by abandoning the factories of America nevertheless thirst for our love by branding the buildings we look at. They want us to honor them for their wealth. Or are they just rubbing it in?

Perhaps the most galling name one frequently sees on new museum galleries or rooms is that of a family that created the opiate epidemic in the United States. This family created an addictive drug that they pushed for decades, convincing doctors and hospitals that the drug was not addicting—knowing all the time that it was. When the company's representatives would report aback to headquarters that doctors had become alarmed by symptoms of addiction in their patients who were taking this company's drugs, the representatives were sent back to convince the doctors and hospitals that those symptoms were not of addiction but of not having ENOUGH of the drug!

They encouraged doctors to put the people showing signs of addiction on more powerful doses—and, of course, at higher prices.

Criminals—who now want us to love them as respectable "patrons of the arts."

We ourselves over the years have already paid for those museums and libraries many times over with a cacophony of public assistance in one form or another. Perhaps the land was donated by the city or by someone who was given some other benefit by the city—all with our tax money. Then the museum lives tax free as a charity. More of our tax dollars come into play when rich people for their own tax plans make tax-deductible donations to the museum.

The museums owe their existence to our penny, so why hassle us now with their fees? Their greed is self-defeating. The higher the fee, the fewer people come. That raises the question: Who is the museum for, anyway? Why have they been given tax breaks? We are paying for those museums as taxpayers as much as those with names on the rooms. So why now try to squeeze more pennies out of us?

Researching Ancestors Plan

When I was at Calvary Cemetery's office making arrangements for the burial of my brother, Big Jimmy, I noticed a number of people coming in and asking questions about long-ago burials. These people were old—very old, for the most part. Seems that searching out the details of one's ancestors becomes a natural curiosity as you get older. Let's make it a Plan.

I think if I tell you the story of my own family research, it will give you some ideas of how you can make out a Ten-Year Plan.

In 1998, for various reasons I found myself with time on my hands. As a hobby I began researching how my pioneering ancestors had taken that leap of faith to escape the grinding poverty of Southern Italy to cross the Atlantic on ships to plant their families in the New World.

Back in 1998 there was not much information on the internet and few, if any, ancestry research sites. Today the scene is very different, and much can be obtained on the internet.

I remember how much of a kick I got out of finding what looked like one of my ancestors on a ship in the 1880s or '90s going back and forth between Italy and the United States. People were traveling on steamships by that time, and the voyage took anywhere from nine to sixteen days, depending on the weather and the steamship itself. Conditions for emigrants improved considerably during that time, from steerage (cargo spaces between decks) to third-class cabins.

The German ships were more expensive but had a much better reputation for safety, cleanliness, and comfort than the Italian ships. When my great-grandfather on my mother's side, Carmine Maffei, finally took his entire family—wife, four children at that time, and his father—to America, he even traveled first from his hometown in Southern Italy, Atripalda, Naples, all the way up to Genoa in Northern Italy to catch the German steamship *Kaiser Wilhelm II.*

At first just the men came. You can tell so much about what was going on just by seeing how they traveled, whom they traveled with, whom they met at the port, where they claimed to be heading. All our stories are different, but on both sides of my family, the men who led the pilgrimages were mature men, artisans (a barber and a tailor) who had already started their families in small towns or villages just outside Naples, one in Casoria and the other in Atripalda, before testing the world on the other side of the Atlantic.

You can imagine the debates and decisions that had to be made between husbands and wives, parents, grandparents, and children during the several years when the men were traveling back and forth to the US. It would be momentous—uprooting families from their ancestral land. What had the men found over there? Was there enough work to support a family? What was it like? Were the people nice? Eventually the decision was to bring over the wife and children. Then the American Experience began.

As it must happen in most cases, the inspiration to find your roots would come after your parents are gone. So it was in my case. The most valuable sources, parents and grandparents, are gone, and for the most part, they left few records or pictures. They had more pressing things to do.

As I remember it now, I started with a few documents, primarily those that my mother had kept. There was her birth certificate, her father's naturalization papers, my father's naturalization certificate, and their marriage license. Funny how in reviewing my experience now, I realize that indeed the first step outside did start at the end—the cemeteries where those pioneers were buried. It involved reading inscriptions of dates of births and deaths; who else was buried with them; obituaries giving details of survivors, funeral homes, parish churches that held the funeral mass, and so on. I visited those churches and found out who had made the preparations. I examined the tombstones in New Jersey, Queens, and Brooklyn.

As I traced back from there, the next big area of research was when and how the first of them had come to the United States, the land of opportunity. In 1998 you had to go to some government office or a big library to look at the films containing information on ships arriving in the United States from Europe. I remember visiting the National Archives unit in New York City. At that time, it was located on an upper floor of a grand old building on Varick Street in Manhattan. It has since been moved to the renovated Customs House at Bowling Green in Manhattan.

Today most of your work will be on the internet. There are scores of scoundrels who show up on any Google search offering to help you find your ancestors, so, as in anything on the internet, you have to be careful and wade through a lot of junk. But you cannot go wrong by starting with the Ellis Island website and the (free) "Family Search" website of the Church of Latter-Day Saints, commonly known at the Mormons. The Mormons, for their own religious reasons, have pioneered the collection of records, worldwide, of people's births. Some of their records are not yet processed for the internet but can be accessed at annexes to some of their church locations. I recently made some very pleasant visits to one such Mormon location in Toms Rivers, New Jersey, to search records of Italian towns from the 1800's.

My Mother's Side-Maffei

My mother was born on Union Street in Brooklyn in 1905 and baptized at the Parrocchia della Madonna della Pace on Carroll Street, now called the Church of Our Lady of Peace. That church was founded in 1898 by Italian missionary priests called the Vicentians, an order descended from St. Vincent DePaul to serve the burgeoning Italian immigrant community in South Brooklyn. The church itself was erected in 1904, the year before my mother was born.

At that time all its priests were Italian (first Vincentians, then Franciscans), its records were kept in Italian, and all the ceremonies, including masses, were in Italian.

My mother's baptismal name was Giuseppa Maffei, and she was the daughter of Ippolito Maffei and Luisa Cioffi. When my mother herself later got married in the same church in 1926, her first name was listed as Giuseppina. When I was growing up, she was always Josephine or Josie to her friends.

Her father was a barber by the name of Ippolito Maffei, also called James, one of thirteen children of Carmine Maffei and Giuseppina Biondi. Ippolito's father, my mother's grandfather, Carmine, also a barber, was the pioneer of the family.

Apparently the Maffei brothers, Carmine, Generoso, Sabino (Samuel), and Lorenzo (Lawrence), had made several trips between the United States and Italy in the early 1890s. In 1896, at the age of forty, Carmine finally brought over his wife and four of their young children on the *Kaiser Wilhelm II*. Ippolito, his oldest son and my grandfather, had already arrived in the United States the year before at the age of thirteen with one of his uncles, also on the *Kaiser Wilhelm II*.

Carmine must have been a vigorous character. He obtained his US citizenship in 1900, giving his residence as 45 Front Street in Brooklyn. In the same year, he and Ippolito, now James, were listed in a Manhattan business directory as Maffei & Son, Barbers, at 169-Park Row. That listing continued through 1905.

When I discovered this fact, I got pretty excited. Park Row in 1900 was the center of the publishing world, with great buildings lining the street just across from city hall. It was indeed a part of the City that Never Sleeps, as publishers, reporters, and newsboys were out and about all day and night.

There was the World Building, also known as the Pulitzer Building; the New York Tribune Building; the New York Times Building; and the Potter building—all on Park Row.

I imagined my great-grandfather and my grandfather hobnobbing with the giants of the newspaper world, or at least with fascinating reporters and politicians moving in and out of their barber shop at 169 Park Row and sharing all the news and gossip of the day. I could see the great publisher Joseph Pulitzer wandering into my ancestors' shop for a haircut and shave. Carmine would have said to him, "Bon giorno, my good sir, glada to seea you. Whatsa your name?"

Pulitzer would answer, "I am Joseph Pulitzer, and I work just down the block."

Carmine would eye him suspiciously and ask, "Wella, Signore Pullizza, what parta Italy is youa familia froma?"

I quickly visited the New York Historical Society to look at its collection of turn-of-the-twentieth-century New York City photographs to see if I could find one that showed their barber shop on Park Row in 1900. While I got incredibly close—photographs of the Park Row block just across the street from 169 in 1918—I did not find a photo of their storefront. These photos are from 1918 and show a block of Park Row, with the elevated train tracks above, across the street at around 170 to 180 Park Row.

This certainly doesn't look like the center of the exciting publishing world. I soon learned that Park Row is a very long street in Manhattan and that the great newspaper buildings were at one end, just across from city hall, while at the other end was a not-so-glamorous Manhattan street in the shadows of an El. It all began to make more sense as I learned that this part of Park Row was just a block away from Mott and Mulberry Streets, Little Italy.

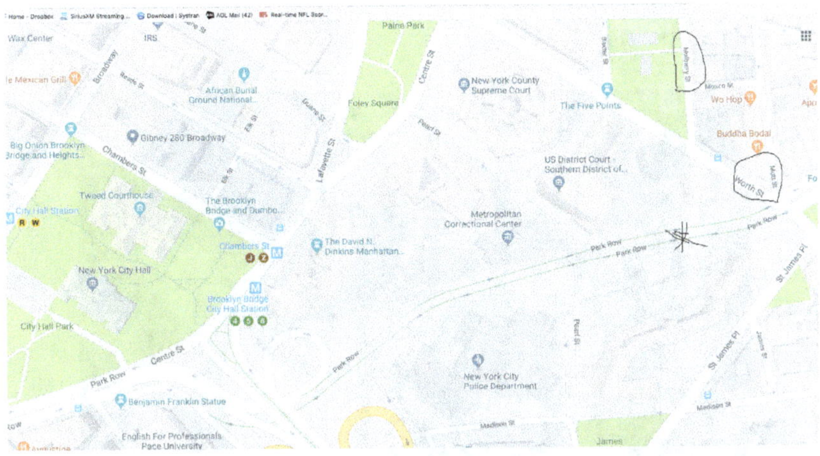

Carmine and Ippolito at that time both lived in South Brooklyn and must have taken the train each day from Brooklyn, over the Brooklyn Bridge and right to Park Row on the other side of the bridge. That would have been an easy commute.

There was a hub for trains from Brooklyn a little farther down on Park Row. This is a photo by the W. C. White Company taken in 1903, when Maffei & Son were in business on Park Row, with the caption "Evening Crowds on Park Row flocking to the Brooklyn Bridge."

Some barber shops in those days.

Sometime just before 1910, Carmine, Giuseppa, their younger children, and his father, Polisto, migrated all the way to Upper Manhattan's Little Italy on East 107th Street near First Avenue.

My grandfather Ippolito, the "Son" of Park Row's "Maffei & Son, Barbers," remained in Brooklyn where he married Luisa Cioffi in 1904 and where their daughter Josephine, my mother, was born on in 1905. He continued to practice as a barber at various locations in Brooklyn. This is a picture of the Federal League Barber Shop at 259 Fourth Avenue, just a couple of blocks away from the homes of my ancestors on Fourth Avenue.

One can date the picture to somewhere between 1912 to 1914 because they were the only years that the Federal League existed. That league was created in 1912 to compete with the two major leagues at the time, the American and National Leagues. The Brooklyn team of the Federal League moved into Washington Park baseball stadium, which had been vacated by the Brooklyn Dodgers in 1912 for Ebbets Field in Flatbush. Washington Park had a seating capacity of 18,000 and was located a block and a half from this barber shop, going in the opposite direction from where my relatives lived, on a large plot of land bounded by First and Third Streets and Third and Fourth Avenues.

Some closer shots of the people at the Federal Barber Shop.

According to the 1910 census, Carmine by that time had reinvented himself into a "grocery retail merchant." His store was just downstairs and next door on 107th Street between First and Second Avenues. It was a family affair, as the grocery store also employed as salesladies his wife, now called Josephine, and two of their six daughters still living at home, Mary, seventeen, and Millie, nineteen.

But the next year, much sadness arrived at the doorstep of Carmine Maffei's family. It seems that at this point, the upward trajectory of this enterprising immigrant had peaked.

On October 10, 1911, Josephine passed away at the age of forty-seven, perhaps soon after the delivery of another child who did not survive her. The cause of death given on her death certificate is "pleurisy with effusion, broncho pneumonia."

Then, as in "When it rains, it pours," just forty days later, Carmine's father, Polisto, passed away at the age of eighty-four, his cause of death being given as "chronic bronco pneumonia."

Polisto, also known as Ippolisto and Modestino, had been born in Atripalda in 1827, married Carmela Catarina in 1855, and had with her the only children he would have, six of them, our Carmine being the oldest. Polisto's occupation in the commune of Atripalda was that of a blacksmith. His first wife died, as did his second, Carmela Melillo, as well as his third, Maria Sabina Carrino. Eventually, at least four of his five sons, as adults, emigrated to the United States. He himself, in 1896 at the quite ripe age for that time of sixty-nine, embarked to the Land of Opportunity.

Our Carmine sadly purchased a double grave and a large tombstone in Calvary Cemetery, a Catholic cemetery in Queens run by the Archdiocese of New York. A double grave means that it could have accommodated six people. It seems he expected this place to serve as a family burial plot for the future. That is confirmed by the size of the tombstone he purchased, with the inscriptions for his father and wife taking up less than a third of its face. There he buried his wife, his father, and an infant child.

The inscription Carmine had carved into the tombstone about his wife always struck me as curious:

Qui Riposa La Mia Adorata Moglie Giuseppina Maffei, Nata 1864
Morta 1911 Lascia Il Desolato Marito con 10 Figli
Lascia il desolato Marito con 10 figlie.
She leaves her desolated husband with 10 children.

Is he complaining? It sounds as if he had ten minors on his hands.

Giuseppa had borne thirteen or fourteen children. He certainly could not consider himself blameless if she died, worn out at forty-seven with yet another infant. The year before in the census, she is listed as working in the grocery store as a saleslady. I wonder if he had her working in his store downstairs while she was pregnant and at the same time caring for the young ones upstairs.

Then there is the number of children that he uses to bemoan his fate: ten. In the census the year before, there are only eight children at home. But there were two others who must have been living at home but for some reason were not there when the census taker made his rounds. There was Anthony, sixteen at the time of the census in 1910, and Peter, three years old. That makes the ten children that he was complaining about.

But of those ten children still at home when his wife died the next year in 1911, three of them were older girls: Mary, eighteen; Lucy, twenty-three; and Millie, twenty. A fourth daughter, Josephine, was fourteen and did not require much minding. The son Anthony was now seventeen and probably working.

Thus, the three older daughters were already in the working world and could be expected easily to take care of the remaining four little ones: Jennie, twelve; Nellie, eight; Peter, four; and Augustine, three.

It seems to me that my great-grandfather, Carmine, instead of complaining about being abandoned by Josephine, could just as well have thanked her for leaving him so well provisioned with wage earners and female caretakers.

At least Carmine did not put any of his four minor children into an orphanage, a practice that was not uncommon due to the lack of any government safety nets at the time. You needed to work every day, or your children would starve.

Nevertheless, Carmine did soon provide his children with a stepmother. On January 22, 1914, the fifty-eight-year-old Carmine married the fifty-six-year-old widow Francesca Canullo Pagnotta, a resident of DeGraw Street, at Our Lady of Peace Church on Carroll Street in Brooklyn. Note how his family ties, though he was now living in upper Manhattan, were still based in downtown Brooklyn.

Before we leave this scene, a word about the great tombstone Carmine purchased in 1911.

Seventy years later, when my father's health was declining in 1984, my mother started looking for a place where he and she could be buried. She had remembered as a child her father taking her to Calvary to visit the grave of his mother. In the thirties, someone from the Maffei family in New Jersey had offered my mother the deed to that Calvary plot, but my mother and her mother were spooked by the idea of a cemetery plot when the family was so young and growing. They rejected the offer out of hand.

Now, fifty years later, she was going around with hat in hand, searching for the deed to that plot. She and my sister Mary Ann went to Red Bank to visit some of her Maffei cousins and asked about the deed. Unfortunately, no one had any idea of what happened to it.

My brother Jerry, retired from the police force, was driving for a funeral service and often made stops at Calvary. Mother asked Jerry to keep his eye out for that tombstone. Jerry, of course, told her he would do so, but he thought to himself that it was silly even to suggest that he could find one plot in that huge cemetery.

Finally, my mother came up with a plan. She would visit a tombstone sales office next to the cemetery and ask them to help her find the plot.

So one day when I was visiting from Dallas, where I had been living, she, my sister Mary Ann, and I drove to the cemetery and looked for a monument seller. We saw a Fasolino Memorials store right next to Calvary and drove into its parking lot. We all walked into the little office, and like some scene from the movies, as soon as my mother saw this Fasolino, she stretched out her arms and exclaimed, "Fasolino!"

And he in turn cried, "Josie!"

It turned out that they knew each other as kids in downtown Brooklyn. Indeed, her mother had taken in this Frank Fasolino for a while when he was very young and had just lost his mother.

Mother asked Frank if he knew how we could find her family's gravesite. Easy enough, he said; let's just go ask. Pretty silly it seems now, but that was all it took. We walked over to the cemetery office and soon located the Maffei plot. My mother said that once we saw the stone, she remembered it exactly as it had been when her father used to take her there, some seventy years earlier. The other thing we noticed when looking at the tombstone was that at the bottom left corner, there was inscribed in very small letters the name of the tombstone's seller: Fasolino.

There was some paperwork to be filled out and some money to be paid, but over the next thirty years, we made good use of Carmine's plot. We buried my father there the next year, in 1986; my mother in 1995; my sisters Louise and Susan in 2013; and finally, my brother Jimmy in 2018.

Soon after Carmine remarried in 1914, he moved out to Jersey, where some of his other children lived, as did two of his brothers and their large and flourishing families.

In 1920 he and his wife, Frances, were living with three of their children, Anthony, Jennie, and Augustine, at 29 Palmer Street in Elizabeth. At sixty-four, Carmine reinvented himself again as a "bridge tender" and worked at the Ferry House, as did his twenty-five-year-old son, Anthony.

Sometime in the thirties, Carmine and Frances moved again, this time to live with their daughter's family, Jennie and Tom Mazzaroppi, on Herbert Street in Red Bank. He passed away at eighty-three in 1939. Frances followed him the next year.

Ironically, particularly in light of that great tombstone he had erected in Calvary in 1911 with his family name carved in large letters, the stone over Carmine's remains in Red Bank's Mount Olivet Cemetery is more modest and curiously has his last name spelled WRONG! Inscribed in stone is the name Carmine Maff**ie**, not Maff**ei.**

I do not know how that could have happened. He did not die alone. His obituary has his name spelled properly and mentions a good number of family members attending the funeral.

In 1998 I visited the church in Red Bank from which he was buried, St. Anthony of Padua on Bridge Avenue, as well as the cemetery office at Mount Olivet. In all of their records concerning the funeral and burial in 1939, he is Carmine Maffei. I noted that his own daughters made the arrangements for the burial. Yet his name is spelled wrong on his tombstone! I checked with the cemetery office and persuaded a lady there to allow me to change the name on the tombstone to agree with the records in her own office. I even got an estimate from some company of what it would cost, about $700 or $1,200 as I remember it now, but I never went any further with it.

On the other hand, when I think about it now, I suspect Carmine himself would not have minded very much, if at all, about the mix-up. After all, Maffei was not even his name. But I will get to that in a moment.

First, I want to mention that this casual attitude toward the family name was shared by at least one of Carmine's own sons, Samuel, who is buried only yards from him in Mount Olivet Cemetery. Sam had created another version of their family name just for himself. He changed his name to Maffe at any early age, as that was how he was listed at twenty-one years old in 1918 with the US Army, where he served as a sergeant in World War I.

Take another look at Sam's tombstone. He died in 1943. It is now 2018. Notice anything?

That picture contains yet another somber story that I have seen reflected in numerous other tombstones over the years. It is a snapshot of people's visions taken at a sad and vulnerable moment.

Sam died in 1943 at the youthful age of forty-six. But he left behind an even more youthful wife, thirty-year-old Althea Mae (Kimmerer). Sam must have met Althea Mae in her hometown of Allentown, Pennsylvania, where the 1930 census has him working in a hospital. They married in Manhattan in 1931 but had no children by the time he died. When the family erected the tombstone, Althea Mae, or someone else, must have envisioned that one day she would be resting beside him, as that blank framed rectangle on the tombstone would indicate. That was not what the future held.

It seems that while the young widow continued to live for a time with the family of Sam's brother Peter, who operated Pete's Barber Shop in Red Bank, she eventually moved on and remarried. She passed away four decades later, in 1984, back in her hometown of Allentown under the name Althea Zehnich.

On the other hand, while we can fully understand why that rectangular box next to Sam's name will forever remain blank, it is difficult to understand why Carmine has remained alone under his misspelled tombstone.

His wife of twenty-five years, Frances, died just a year later, and according to the obituary, she had been living, as Carmine had, with their daughter Jennie's family on Herbert Street. Yet she is buried in Mount Olivet, not with Carmine, but rows and rows of tombstones away, all by herself. What was going on?

Getting back to the family name, it turns out that Carmine's original family name was not Maff**ei**, but Maff**eo**. Their surname in Atripalda for centuries had been and still is Maffeo. In addition, in what I had always ignored as an official's clumsy error, his and his children's last names on the ship manifest on their arrival in 1896 was written as Maffeo. Yet in America he decided to be known as Maffei.

I do not know what got Carmine and his brothers, who also adopted the nomenclature of Maffei, to change, even though subtly, their last name. The only possible clue I happen to notice is that in the 1890s, there was a well-known aristocratic Maffei family in Milan that was frequently in the news. One Count Maffei was the Italian ambassador to Queen Victoria's Court in Great Britain. Another Count Maffei was in the news for his escapades in Monte Carlo, including at least one duel.

Whatever.

My Father's Side-Paone

Raffaele Paone, my grandfather on my father's side, traveled back and forth between Italy and America as Carmine Maffei did. I believe he was doing this in the 1890s, but the only concrete evidence I have is for trips in 1901, 1904, and 1905. He traveled on Italian ships from Naples, and the manifests listed him as a tailor.

I am now residing in a town called Belmar, which is on the Jersey Shore. It takes about two hours to drive up to Bethlehem, Pennsylvania. I made that trip twice last month to see if I could find any trace of my grandfather Raffaele Paone.

I learned some years ago from examining ship manifests that Raffaele gave immigration officials at the Port of New York addresses in Bethlehem as his residences in 1903 and then again in 1905, when he was forty years old. It is very likely that he was in Bethlehem from 1901 to 1907. His younger brother Ciro was with him from 1903.

I did not focus on this short, early period of his time in the United States because his subsequent stay in Red Bank, New Jersey, with his family and then his final destination of Brooklyn, where he spent the rest of his life, attracted more of my attention.

Because Bethlehem is famous as a steel town, I always assumed that he must have worked in the steel mills along with his brother Ciro. He was working like all the other immigrants wherever he could to make some money, perhaps with the intention of bringing his family over.

There are today still many signs of Bethlehem's steel-producing past, though the town, now a delightful and flourishing place, has converted a number of its old factories to useful venues.

But recently, the more I thought about it, the less I could envision my grandfather in a steel mill. As I remember him in his old age, he was still an erect man and something of a dandy. He just did not look like anyone who had ever worked in a steel mill at any time of his life, not that there is anything wrong with such honest labor. But it seemed to me that such work would have been too physical for my grandfather.

In addition, he did repeatedly describe himself as a tailor to the immigration authorities. So why not take him at his word?

Bethlehem was founded in 1741 by the Moravians. "Moravian" denotes both a people and a religion. The Moravians were from an area called Moravia in what is now the Czech Republic and were a Protestant denomination noted for its tolerance. When they settled in the Lehigh Valley, they set up a self-sufficient town with industrial plants on the Monocacy Creek off the Lehigh River to sustain themselves, including grist mills, butcheries, ironsmiths, candlemakers, tanneries, dyes, and the like, with large iron foundries soon to follow.

I found that the old Moravian Cemetery on Market Street, a thoroughfare with old mansions and fine townhouses where the owners and managers of the later industries used to live, included graves of Native Americans and Africans who at death were part of the Moravian church. There were also graves of women and men missionaries who had gone south to spread the faith. I have to assume that my grandfather, having crossed the Atlantic Ocean, certainly must have wandered up to the cemetery sometime during the seven or so years he was there and saw the same mansions and graves that we see now.

Here are some of the finer homes that the owners and managers lived in as they appear today.

On Market Street the Moravians have carefully preserved their old cemetery.

In 1901 the three boroughs of Bethlehem, West Bethlehem, and South Bethlehem had a total population of about twenty-four thousand. They had a large number of immigrants from all the countries of Europe, who were recruited to work in the factories. But who recruited Raffaele, and why to Bethlehem?

There was an Italian community in the far east of South Bethlehem, as each new immigrant group established itself to the east of the earlier arrivals. The Italians, like all the prior groups, built a church at 826 E. Fourth Street in 1902. It was first called Our Lady of the Rosary and later Our Lady of Pompeii. It was a modest church compared to those already established by the Moravians, Episcopal, Germans, Irish, and various Slavic groups.

HOLY INFANCY SCHOOL

When I visited Bethlehem last month, I found out that the Italian church had been closed and the property sold to the Hispanic Baptist Church of Bethlehem. After a little research, I reached a lady at another Catholic church, a much more substantial one that had been founded by German Catholics, and she told me that the records of Our Lady of Pompeii were being stored in their basement. She promised to search for any record of Raphael Paone around the period of 1903, but she was ultimately unable to find anything. Neither was the local librarian able to find any trace of my grandfather.

At the time my grandfather was in Bethlehem, Charles Schwab was just getting ready to leave Carnegie Steel and take over a little iron-and-railroad company in Bethlehem. So it was not Schwab and Bethlehem Steel that brought my grandfather to Bethlehem.

I studied the industries that were flourishing in 1900s Bethlehem, and I am convinced that it was the silk mills that brought him there. Italians already were migrant workers to the great silk centers of Europe, such as Lyon, France, and Bologna, Italy, where they worked on a seasonal basis and then returned home. America was just a little farther, and Pennsylvania, particularly the Lehigh Valley, was teeming with silk mills.

Raffaele was a tailor by trade, and I know that he was in the garment business for the rest of his life. Therefore, he must have been drawn to Bethlehem by one of the silk factories that existed at the time. The addresses that he gave to the immigration officials at the time, 20 W. Third Street and 408 New Street in south Bethlehem, were not next to the steel mills and in fact were not even in the Italian community of the time.

There was, however, the Bethlehem Silk Mill on W. Goepp Street, which would not have been far from where he lived. Back then, most commuting would have been by foot or horse. So I conclude that he was working in the Bethlehem Silk Mill during those years.

This is what the silk mill in Bethlehem looks like today. It has been the subject of various attempts to repurpose it but has not yet found a new life.

It is easier to figure out what Raffaele did next in America.

On August 2, 1907, at the Port of New York, Raffaele met some very special passengers disembarking from the Italian steamship ship *Calabria* after a sixteen-day voyage from Naples, Italy: Francesca Palmigiano, thirty-three, his wife, and Candia Paone, ten; Antonio Paone, eight; and my father, Luciano Paone, six, their children.

He immediately took the family from the port to their new home in a town even smaller than Bethlehem—namely, Red Bank, New Jersey, at that time having a population of about six thousand people. We even have an address for them: 31 Bridge Avenue.

Now, why was he bringing them there?

It is now 1907, and the last time we spied him was in 1905 in Bethlehem. In two years' time, he traveled from Bethlehem to this smaller town on the Jersey Shore and was able to set up a home for his arriving family.

While I have no clue as to how he learned of Red Bank or of job opportunities there, I am sure of one thing: he had found out about the fabulously successful clothing manufacturer Sigmund Eisner.

Eisner was a child when he arrived in America in the 1870s from Bohemia. There were relatives who helped get him on his feet, and he was soon traveling in New Jersey as a peddler. On one of those trips, he arrived in Red Bank and met a lady, Bertha Weis, the daughter of a family he was staying with. They eventually married, and he settled in her hometown. Together they started to produce clothing for sale from their home with their two sewing machines.

It did not take long for Sigmund to focus on the uniform market as his main enterprise. With careful management of resources and using the latest sewing machines, he was able to outbid competitors and become a favorite of the US military, who used his uniforms in the Spanish-American War. His uniforms were spread around the world by the Boy Scouts, park rangers, US Marines, and US nurses.

By the time Raffaele arrived in 1907, Eisner had begun to construct his ultimate plant on Bridge Street, a complex that would become the largest and most modern uniform manufacturing facility in the United States, and Eisner would produce millions of uniforms for the US military during World War I.

Eisner established a state-of-the-art factory, with workers organized by their special functions and using the latest machinery. He was proud to claim that he had produced the best environment for his workers of any factory up to that time, with plenty of space and much light from windows and overhead lamps. His plans for the factory became a blueprint for garment factories of the future, including that of my grandfather and father down the road.

These pictures of his factory workers remind me of my father and uncle's shop, except that instead of having men predominately working in their factory, as Eisner did, my grandfather and father hired primarily women to work on sewing machines, while the pressers were men.

I have been over to the sixteen-room Victorian home that was Sigmund's last, at 84 W. Front Street in Red Bank, and asked if they had any employment records from 1907 or so. The Eisner home is now the main Red Bank Library and houses the records of the Eisner family. No, they did not have any employment records.

I was not surprised, as it was a long time ago and things just do not stay the same.

Nearly all his workers were hardworking Italian and Polish immigrants. One major key to his success was their industrious habits and low wages. To keep those wages low—or, in his view, reasonable—he endured a number of difficult strikes, doggedly resisting unionization in some ugly battles. Like most of the other industrialists in the early twentieth century, he resorted to physical opposition by hiring private guard agencies from out of town as well as out-of-town strikebreakers. At one point he threatened to shut down the plant and move out of Red Bank. That threat won for him the energetic material of the local politicians and the police department in his fight against union organizers, both local and from Philadelphia and New York. Thus he was able to continue to outbid competitors time and time again for the government contracts.

He had produced a magnificent factory with plenty of room and light for his workers, the best at the time, but he was not going to lose his competitive edge by overpaying them. Neither would Walmart or Amazon think of doing such in the future. Though he would provide housing for some workers and was generally considerate, often calling the workers his family, he had to keep his wages as low as possible to win his bids. For the immigrant worker, those wages were more than sufficient, and he was never in want of people to operate his factory.

Sigmund died in 1925, and eventually the grand factory closed, fell into disuse, and deteriorated.

Happily, those buildings have found a new life today as the Galleria, a very handsome renovation with offices, shops, and restaurants.

Now, back to my grandfather in 1907.

You recall I said that he settled the family at 31 Bridge Avenue. While I have not checked the records, I doubt that he owned the building, and I must assume he rented an apartment there.

But the crucial fact is that only a block away on Bridge Avenue stood the Sigmund Eisner factory! Now, it does not take much speculation to conclude that this tailor who lived a block away would be working at this clothing factory. You remember from the pictures of his workers that most of the people at those sewing machines were male.

This is the house at 31 Bridge Avenue, thanks to Google Maps.

Then it is a short walk up Bridge Avenue to the Eisner factory / Galleria.

GALLERIA
Bridge Ave
Google

GALLERIA

His wife, Francesca, stayed home with the children, and we see from the June 30, 1909, edition of the Red Bank Register that the Paone children were moving along in the public school system.

OAKLAND STREET SCHOOL.

Promoted to 2d grade from 1st grade —Margaret Demmert, Edna Burke, Emilia Pace, Geraldine Wenzell, Alice Sherman, Elizabeth Richardson, Anita Riddle (moved to Holmdel), Verna Pittenger, Lucy Valentine, Marion Scott, Marion Frey, Lida Emmons, Loretta Conover, Charlotte Bottlcher, Milton Earle, William Cavano, Kenneth Walker, Luciano Paone, Herbert Williams, Robert VanDusen, Charles VanKelst, Harry Rice, Henry Ratana, Antonio Paone, Benjamin Greenburg, William Egolf, George Dunbar, Fred Colmorgen, Howard Chamberlain, James Bennett, Charles Allaire, Kenneth Adcock, Charles Tindall, Pautelene Polette, Benjamin Johnson, Harvey Gaunt.

Promoted to 4th grade from 3d grade —Harold Brasch, Robert Cooper, Fred Frick, Francis Higgins, Meyer Lipack, James Nicoletti, Charles Otterson, Hugh Phillips, Harry Sherman, George Silver, Benjamin Tilton, Joseph Talerico, Franklin Weller, Harold Johnson, George Toombs, Velenah Carver, Theressa Conover, Gertrude Dorowitz, Lillian Lewis, Beatrice Munsell, Candita Paone, Lena Sole, Matilda Demmert.

We can assume that while in Red Bank, Raffaele lived a thrifty life and saved enough money to stake himself to a little shop of his own, a baby Eisner factory. But of course, he could not do that in the small town of Red Bank, so they moved on.

My father must have remembered fondly the few years he spent in Red Bank as a child, because in his later years, he once asked to be driven down to Red Bank to take a look around. He showed us the spot in the river where they used to go swimming—it is still accessible by way of a small park on the side of the Red Bank Library, Eisner's old home. We went by where he had lived and stopped at a diner where the family sometimes used to eat.

We next find Raffaele and his family finally arriving in Brooklyn in October 1910. They set up in an apartment at 181 Fourth Avenue between DeGraw and Sackett Streets, joining the folks who had arrived earlier on Little Italy's Fourth Avenue and who would one day be relatives by marriage, the Cioffi family from Maddaloni, Italy, at 209 and 228 Fourth Avenue, and a member of the Maffei family from Atripalda at 201 Fourth Avenue, between Sackett and Union Streets.

My mother would tell us how as a child she would bathe at the public bathhouse on Fourth and President, as apparently the apartment buildings on Fourth Avenue around 1905 did not have baths.

This is a photo of her bathhouse as it looks today. Thanks to having been designated a national historic monument and also a NYC landmark, its exterior has been preserved.

It was called New York City's Public Bath No. 7, the last and most decorative that the city erected. It was put up in 1907, just when the urgent need for public baths declined. At around the same time, the city passed laws requiring apartment buildings to have indoor showers or baths, making the public baths much less necessary.

Recently it has been cleaned up and put to a new use as a fitness center, just as the surrounding area is sustaining a phenomenal building boom, changing the character of the neighborhood forever, for better or worse.

She also mentioned that when she was a little girl, she and her friends would lie down on the ventilation grates in the middle of Fourth Avenue in the summer to catch the cooling breezes of passing subway trains. This must have been later, perhaps when the family had already moved off Fourth Avenue to larger quarters at the corner of Sackett and Fifth, because the BMT's Fourth Avenue subway line did not yet exist in 1905.

This is what the subway grates on Fourth Avenue look like today. They seem narrower than what I remember. Perhaps the city did not think the subway needed that much air or that the air outside was more polluted than that underground. Anyway, I can't imagine children lying on those grates today to get refreshing breezes. They would have to dodge much heavier and faster vehicle traffic and then endure only putrid air coming up from the tunnels beneath.

There is a company that sells old photos of New York City on the internet, Brooklynpic.com. I don't know how they came across their inventory. They don't give names for the photographers, for the most part, yet they claim to have copyrights to these old pictures, which I doubt very much. There is no identification of the photographer or the original company that had the photo taken—those who would have had the copyrights, if any. Well, whatever. But they have good prints of the photos, and I could not possibly resist buying at least one of their prints, which just happens to capture Raffaele's home on Fourth Avenue while his family was there.

Here is a picture of the building that Raffaele moved into on Fourth Avenue. Note the address over the door of the building on the right, 181. The picture's seller put a date of 1919 on the photo, but I don't think they really know. Let's say it is around the time my grandfather and his family lived there, from around 1910 to 1915.

Note the building number over the door on the right.

Is that my grandmother shopping downstairs?

Or is Grandma that shadow in the window upstairs, watching the street?

Could this be my father with a relative or neighborhood child on his shoulders? And whose face is that in the window under the hanging cheeses?

Next door at 179 is a furniture shop advertising that they also repair stoves!

Today that building is still standing, though barely, and it apparently is even occupied, but I can't imagine who would want to live there in the middle of what is going on around it. The present owner of this old three-story building is probably a speculator trying to push out some rent-controlled tenants so he or she can sell the building to the manic builders swarming over the neighborhood.

There is an advertising sign in front of the excavated lots next door that describes what will replace the three-story buildings—yet another glass-faced twelve-plus-story "luxury" apartment building.

For a moment, let's stay with the above "Work in Progress" advertisement. Note that the seller has this glass tower flanked by attractive old-neighborhood three-story buildings.

A lie.

The seller wants the prospective buyers to think they will be moving into a charming and humanly scaled neighborhood, even though they themselves will be living in that glass box. In reality those quaint three-story buildings that the seller is using to promote his glass tower are the very buildings that are being demolished by this seller and his fellow developers.

What the seller does not want the prospective buyer to suspect is that the buyer will soon be living in a glass box that will be standing shoulder to shoulder with other glass boxes up and down Fourth Avenue.

Here is a picture of the manic "progress" now going on along Fourth Avenue.

The politicians in the city who like to call themselves "liberal," meaning they are for the "working people," have been playing a duplicitous game.

With one side of their faces, they decry the lack of affordable housing and the cruel indifference to this problem of some higher governmental body—not their own, of course—but with the other side of their faces, they quietly smile upon developer-friendly zoning changes that ignite wildfires chasing middle-income people out of the city.

These pyromaniacs express shock or bewilderment or even anger at the raging fires that they themselves have set—zoning changes that created the inevitable economic dynamic that increases the value of land, attracts developers, and encourages older building owners to sell immediately or set to work forcing out lower-rent or rent-controlled tenants so they can sell an empty building at a higher price. The ugly face of "gentrification" propelled by "liberal" politicians in the city—and probably in most other cities.

This is exactly what is happening with Brooklyn's downtown Fourth Avenue. Many thousands of affordable housing units have vanished—new development pushing our first-, second-, and third-generation Brooklynites to be replaced by Midwesterners or whoever is looking for a place to sleep within easy commuting distance to their cubicles in Manhattan where they will spend their days.

New York's politicians are quick to castigate Trump for selling America's soul to Saudi Arabia for billions of dollars, but they themselves have sold

Brooklyn's soul for peanuts. Incidentally, the odds are that those lower-middle-class people who were chased out of their homes are pretty angry and resentful and have joined that pool of "deplorables" from which Trump has drawn his water.

Ironically, the builders have been attracting renters or condo buyers with pictures of the neighborhood as it used to be and with the promise of a nice subway ride on the BMT Fourth Avenue Line into Manhattan.

But it is all a lie.

The newcomers will find an exciting mixed community but just anxious newcomers like themselves living in identical tall glass boxes, with all of them together literally crushing to death that poor Fourth Avenue subway line—transformed from subway cars to moving sardine cans.

Going back again in my story to my grandparents' day.

This next picture is described as "The Italian Quarter" in the internet photo seller's catalogue. It is of Union Street at Fourth Avenue. I am not confident about the date given by the seller, 1915, because I do not think the BMT subway exit at Union Street shown in the picture existed in 1915. I believe it may have come along a few years later. The neighborhood and its inhabitants certainly had an air of vitality and spark to them.

It seems as if it's a Sunday and everyone is out and talking to someone else, passing the news, asking about families, and so on.

For the fun of it, I went up there this past weekend and took some pictures of what the Fourth and Union intersection looks like today.

As my grandmother used to say, "It's not like it was in the old days."

Upon their move to Brooklyn around 1910, Raffaele and his family would not have felt out of place in their new setting, though it was certainly a lot more crowded and busier than Red Bank was. Aside from this being an Italian neighborhood where you could go all day without encountering anyone speaking English, the city as a whole had an overall foreign, European in particular, influence.

A report at the time by the Federal Industrial Commission estimated that 42 percent of New York City's population was foreign born but that if you added their children, which the commission thought should be considered as foreign as well, then the city had a "foreign element" of 80 percent.

By 1920 everyone—that is, the Paone, Maffei, and Cioffi families—had left Fourth Avenue itself, though not the neighborhood, probably because of the mess caused to the avenue by subway construction. The subway contractors along Fourth Avenue used the open-trench method, digging deep ditches for the tunnel and then temporarily covering them with wood planks for a roadway. Here are some photos of the construction along Fourth Avenue from a contemporary city report.

Excavation south of Seventh Street

Excavation south of Ninth Street

Raffaele, upon arriving in Brooklyn, must have immediately put some of Sigmund Eisner's ideas into practice and opened his own little Eisner factory, except his shop and later that of his sons were always unionized. I speculate that he must have had a factory because by 1920 he was prosperous enough to move his family into a newly built two-family attached brick house at 195 Eighth Street, a good distance in space and value from their previous apartment at 181 Fourth Avenue. This is a view today of 195 Eighth Street.

The 1920 census has Raffaele's wife, Frances, at home as a housewife. But all three children are machinists or tailors working at a "shop," and I am sure it was Raffaele's shop. When we were growing up, we used to call what must have been the successor factory, Paone Brothers Coat Company, my uncle Tony and my father's place on Thirty-Ninth Street, "the Shop."

Just a few years later, in 1925, Raffaele, now sixty, bought a really grand, newly constructed multifamily brownstone at the corner of Sixth Avenue and Lincoln Place, some blocks away but in another world economically. Here are a couple of photos of that building today.

To put a finish to the story of my ancestors, let me show you my grandfather Raffaele years later during a light moment with two of his children, Suzie and Tony, in his sons' shop on Thirty-Ninth Street in Brooklyn.

Raffaele was not able to replicate the greatness of Sigmund Eisner, but he sure as hell tried—and did pretty well for himself, and for us.

Writing Your Biography Plan

Everybody has a story. Why not write your story? You don't have to be afraid that people will learn about your dark secrets—just don't include them in the story you write. Besides, most of the people you may get into trouble with a particular story have already gone to their reward. Remember that it is *your* story. You tell the world whatever you want, nothing more and nothing less. All biographies are that way.

A biography is whatever you make of it. You can trace your life, that of your parents and siblings, your children and grandchildren. This may be the only opportunity you have to really say what you want to say.

There is no reason why your biography shouldn't make you look good. Nor does that pain in the ass you hated all your life deserve to be treated fairly. Dump on them if you wish, with all the imagination you can muster—is it true they embezzled at work? Did they really make that young girl pregnant? They only shower once a month?

Going to Funerals Plan

We eighty-plus folks will know a good number of people who will die during the next decade—bringing sadness when our friends and relatives pass and joy when our enemies finally drop dead. It is hard to say in general on what side the scale will weigh, as each of us has a different number of friends and enemies. I think something of a Plan could be made out of this inevitability.

Over the years, when I have attended wakes, funeral masses, burials, or shivas, I've noticed that a lot of older people were in attendance. At funeral homes, I would see them in the lobby, sitting on sofas, using the bathrooms— they seemed comfortable with their role as ornaments of the last goodbye.

At my father's wake, I remember seeing several older ladies come in to pay their respects. None of us had any idea who they were, and we just assumed they were some long-forgotten acquaintances of my father. My mother, on the other hand, just said cryptically, "Oh, those are the ladies who just go to funerals." While she may have been referring to a particularly Italian custom, I have found about the same thing happening wherever there was a ceremony for the dead. I don't want to analyze why this is the case, but it does tell me that this might be a comfortable and familiar Plan for an eighty-year-old.

First of all, at your age there will be more deaths among your friends and acquaintances than average. You are lucky to have a head start on this Plan. To follow this Plan, you should naturally attend all the related ceremonies— wakes, masses, processions, burials, luncheons, shivas. But you need to be diligent. When someone you know dies, find out when the funeral services and burial will be. Of course, among non-Christians there will be no wake or funeral mass. Jewish and Muslim burials will be swift. So you must also be swift. Upon hearing of a death, immediately call up mutual friends or the deceased's relatives and find out the burial schedule. If you were not close to the family, or perhaps just barely knew the deceased, you may want to keep your enquiries to your mutual friends. Fortunately, if you fail to catch the burial, both Muslims and Jews have a mourning period after death where visitors are welcome.

Whether you drive in burial processions to the cemetery depends on whether you can still drive or have someone drive you there. But it is recommended that you attend as many burials as possible, as the postburial luncheons can be the most satisfying thing under this Plan.

This Plan will require that you go beyond your immediate friends and acquaintances. You can't count on that many of them dying during this ten-year period to keep you fully occupied. This is where the internet comes in handy. Each day, if there is no funeral among your friends, check the obituaries on the internet and find one in your town or nearby. How far you want to travel is up to you. Some may seem more inviting than others. There may be funeral homes or churches you've always wanted to see. A tour of an unfamiliar cemetery may be a reward in itself. You may even decide to put a revisit on a list of things to do in the future—to read the interesting inscriptions more closely.

Don't hesitate to go. Grieving families always welcome condolences and shows of compassion. No one in pain questions a kindly word of comfort.

The Pet Adoption Plan

Animals can bring a world of joy and fun into the lives of eighty-year-olds. But there are some sensible things you need to consider.

First of all, remember your age and plan it so you don't leave your best friend behind to an unknown fate when you are gone. So it is best not to be getting any puppies or kitties when you are eighty unless you are ABSOLUTELY sure you have lined someone up to take the pet in if you leave the picture. In fact, this is a good thing to arrange for any pet you may have.

But it is also easier to take care of a dog that is beyond its wild puppy years. You could get a lovable but mature pet from a shelter. To do it right, you will need to devote yourself to its care. Your devotion will be returned tenfold and make your life full and happy. You will find yourself smiling and laughing at the things you pet does, they are so full of surprises.

I have been blessed with endless rewards for living with dogs and cats. They are fun to be with; you feel their devotion; they bring people-friends along the way; they get me out into a lovely world—but also require me to get outside when I would not otherwise want to, but all ending well. More on my own experiences later.

Now, remember that you have to be able to take care of your pet. In addition, your living conditions must be suitable for pets. If you get a dog or two, you need to walk the dog every day, maybe twice a day. Or find a nearby dog park to take the dogs to. Feeding and vet visits are required, and these will cost some money. Food is not expensive, but the vet visits can be. Presently there is something out of whack with the veterinary world. Why in heaven's name are they so expensive? At any rate, try to shop around and find a good doctor who does not overcharge.

Adopting a friend at eighty-plus is a major undertaking. Don't undertake it lightly—you are not a teenager who can palm off your pet to your parents if it doesn't "work out." Once you take the step you MUST make it work out—you owe it to yourself and the dog or cat. The last thing you want to do is raise the hopes of a dog or cat, get it used to the good life, and then dump it into a shelter or onto an angry and resentful relative.

While I have your attention, let me tell you about the pets in my life. I think you will find my story interesting.

When I was about ten, my brother and sister, Mary Ann and Georgie— the "twins," as that was what they were, born a year after me—campaigned with our parents to get a dog.

My father was inclined to give in to our importuning, but my mother insisted that we could not get a dog while our cat, Tootsie, was still with us. I don't know what sex Tootsie was, but I always assumed the cat was female, I guess from the name. That cat had an enormously powerful position in our family because of an incident a few years earlier. That incident had been elevated to a legend in our family: "The Amazing Story of Tootsie."

Let me just give you that legend as it was written down many years ago in the Secret Annals of the Paone Family.

The cat Tootsie, who was famously camera shy, was photographed in front of our house on 48th Street in Brooklyn with Mary Ann. It must have been a good day for Tootsie, as she was letting Mary Ann pet her.

Tootsie and Mary Ann

Tootsie, who had arrived in the family before Mary Ann, Georgie, and Arthur, had made herself unwelcome to my mother and her mother, our grandmother who was living with us, because she often would scratch the little kids in the family. Daddy was ordered to eliminate the cat.

It is not known what Daddy thought of these instructions, but I am sure he followed the precepts laid down by his ancestors and by which his own mother had raised him.

"You gotta do what you gotta do."

So one dark and wet night, Daddy coaxed the unsuspecting Tootsie into his big black car, promising her a nice ride around town, and took her for a ride.

At that time we were living on Forty-Eighth Street in Brooklyn. Far across Brooklyn was the famous beach resort of Coney Island. That was where Daddy headed with Tootsie. The cat was in shock when they got there, with all the bright lights, loud noises, and freaky places. She had never been to such a place.

But Daddy nevertheless persuaded her to leave the comfort and safety of the big car and go for a little walk with him…

Once they were a few steps from the car, Daddy ran back to the car, jumped in, and gunned the engine, taking off in a hurry. Years later he confessed that he did not even have the courage to look Tootsie in the eye and say goodbye.

Now all alone, being streetwise as she was, and though it was unbelievable, she understood immediately what had happened to her. She began to wander about. People were looking funny at her. They did not seem friendly at all.

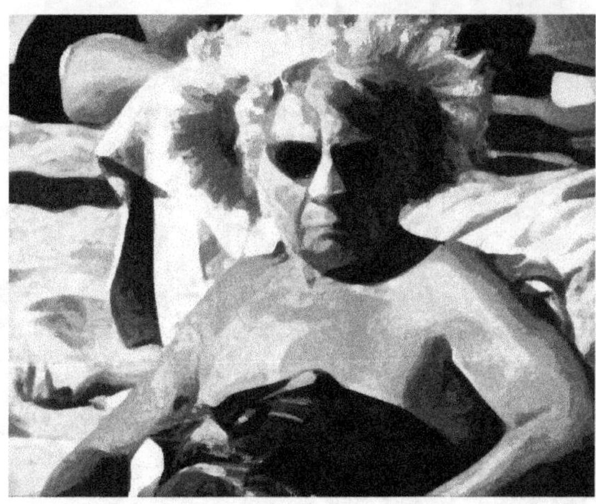

As she walked around the strange place, she thought of home. She even missed the kids. Eventually she found a dark corner, curled up, and cried herself to sleep.

The next morning, she awoke to a maddening scene of millions of people, it seemed, packed like sardines on the sand.

That was when she determined that she was going to find her way back home, no matter what it took. Off she went into the strange and wild streets of Brooklyn, miles and miles of streets—but she always knew which way to go. Something inside told her.

One night many weeks later, Mother and Daddy heard a scratching noise at their bedroom window.

They looked out, and there she was: TOOTSIE! They were stunned, amazed, and also deeply relieved by the sight of the ragged Tootsie. They now had been given a chance to make right what they had done. Tootsie that night became one of their most cherished children.

When grandmother woke up and was told, she exclaimed, "It's a miracle! It's a miracle! It's a miracle!" in three languages, one of them unknown.

Daddy pulled some strings at the Pentagon, and the next day the army paraded down Forty-Eighth Street in honor of Tootsie.

Mother had a statute of Tootsie erected in our backyard and then brought together all the neighbors for a blessing dedication by Father O'Brien.

...and tootsie lived happily ever after at Forty-Eighth Street.

The End!

You can see what we kids were up against. But we kept at it until my father relented, and then, finally, my mother did as well, but only after my father and uncle brought home a cute little puppy that we promptly named Queenie.

Queenie was my first dog. Here is me and then Georgie with Queenie.

The next dog that I could rightfully call my own was Lacey. When my wife, Elaine, and I got a house in Dallas, we felt that a house should have a dog. Elaine already had a pet called Missy, a sweet and lovable cat.

Missy

Because we wanted to make sure that any new pet would get along with our little Missy, we went out and asked about it at some pet stores in Dallas.

Back in 1980 you did not just go to Google to find information. You went out and found somebody with expertise. There were no big-box pet stores back then, but little shops with the owners on these premises, and they actually knew something about animals. In a couple of places, we were told that Shelties, or Shetland Sheepdogs, were mild mannered and most likely to befriend a cat. Thus, little Lacey arrived on the scene.

Lacey

Sure enough, there was no problem between Missy and Lacey. It turned out that Missy was just fearless of new animals and was not in the least jealous when additional members were added to the family—she accepted them all.

A little while later, Elaine and I were window shopping on a Sunday afternoon when we came to a pet shop. We went in to look at the animals and came upon a mildly disturbing scene. There was a big salesperson in a white coat showing off a little puppy to some people. The puppy, a black toy poodle, was so tiny that the salesperson was joking as he put the dog into the various pockets of his coat. Finally, he put the puppy back into the cage, and the poor thing's feet were so tiny that they kept falling through the wire floor of the cage. We both thought that was a little cruel, and we left the place in a bad humor.

The next day at work, I made a command decision and called the pet store. I told the lady on the phone that I wanted to buy that little black toy poodle that I had seen on display the day before.

"Oh," she said, "I am sorry, but someone called before you and placed a hold on it. But we have other puppies that you might be interested in."

"No," I said, happy that the little thing was getting out of that place, "but thank you anyway."

When I got home that night, I found my wife holding the little black toy poodle in her hands! Obviously, great minds think alike. Gigi had arrived.

Gigi

She was welcomed warmly into the family by Missy and Lacey.

Now there were three.

We were lucky in that all of them got along very well. Both Missy and Lacey treated the new puppy like a little sister.

A few years later, I happened to notice that a local dog shelter very close to our house was having an open house to raise money for its operation. They would accept donations in kind, such as dog or cat food, or cash. I decided to drop in on my way from work and make a cash contribution.

Very cleverly—at least I thought so later on—the shelter had its signs for the campaign arranged so that you had to walk through the entire building, past all the dogs and cats in their cages, to get to the front desk to make your contribution.

I steeled myself against any impulse to pick up another animal and walked briskly through the place, but apparently not quickly enough.

There were cages on both sides of the walkway to the front desk, with dogs yapping and howling and barking in their excited reactions to the people flowing through. There were parents with a lot of children, all trying to connect with the animals, making funny noises and poking their fingers into the cages.

Making my way to the front office through this pandemonium, I was halfway there when I sensed a silence to my right.

I glanced over and saw this black dog sitting quietly. It seemed he was in his own world, silently observing the noisy goings-on in front of him, with only his eyes moving.

Now those enchanting eyes seemed to be beckoning to me. I quickly turned my head to the front and willed myself to ignore those magical eyes. Certainly, this was a far different creature from everything else in the building, just calmly sitting there in that chaos and watching the people go by. But I could not afford to get hooked; we already had three pets at home. I soldiered on.

Nevertheless, after making my contribution at the front desk, I was overcome by whatever one gets overcome by in those situations. I asked one of the volunteers to show me that quiet, little black dog.

At each cage there were handwritten notes that briefly described each of the animals in that particular cage. My object of interest was thought to be several months old and had recently been found in the street. But in the same cage was an old dog—I remember it now as a small type of dog, handsome but wizened. The note for that dog was heartbreaking: it had been left at the shelter by its owner, who had loved him for ten years but was no longer able to care for him.

Goodness, I said to myself, it looks like I am going to be getting not just one, but two new friends.

As the volunteer reached in and took out my little black dog, a young boy came racing up to the cage exclaiming, "There, Mom, there he is! That is what I WANT!" Lo and behold, to my great relief, the child was pointing at the older dog. I escaped the place with just one little black dog.

Gus

As I was walking the dog to my car, it became animated, and I thought I saw him actually kick up his heels. At that time, I owned a convertible, and the top was down. I deposited the newest member of our family into the back seat and drove off. As soon as we got rolling, the dog jumped to the top of the back seat, sat down, and looked forward, taking the position of an experienced ship's captain. "Ah, now this is the life. A sucker is born every day!" he seemed to be saying.

Now there were four.

The first week the new dog was with us, he escaped our fenced-in yard three or four times, only to return on his own. I thought I had the yard escape proofed, since neither Gigi nor Lacey nor Missy had ever slipped through the fence. But this new pet seemed to have some extra talents.

Eventually I fixed all the places that seemed to be his escape locations. In the meantime, the dog seemed to be relaxing in his new home. His wanderings around the neighborhood must have convinced him that there was nothing better out there.

But now we knew we had a rascal on our hands. We named him after a scoundrel we had heard about: a stowaway who married an American, was a drunk and a womanizer, had a few children with his wife, and then promptly abandoned them. Hence, our dog's name was Gus.

One day I was in the vet's waiting room for some reason with one of our animals when I noticed a lady with an older dog on a leash. She was talking to the receptionist. I could not hear what they were saying, but something seemed out of the ordinary. The lady left without the dog. Since I was at the vet so often with all our pets, I knew the staff very well. I went up to the assistant who had taken the dog and asked what that was all about. Well, it seemed that the owner thought that this dog was too old, and it was just too much trouble to take care of it anymore. Her daughter had brought it in to be put down.

"For heaven's sake," I said, "this dog looks OK to me. You certainly are not going to put it down. Let me have it."

The vet's assistant apologized but said she had to refuse. Though she agreed with me about it being wrong, she could not give the dog away because the office had an obligation to the person who had brought the dog in. They had to do what they had agreed to do.

That really upset me, and it was not something I would forget.

A year or so later, that scene eerily played out again. While in the same waiting room, I noticed a young woman with a cat in a carrying case come in and chat with the receptionist. Something was funny, but this time I was not going to wait around to find out the bad news. I approached them and said something or other to get myself involved in the conversation.

Bottom line: the woman was a stewardess and was frequently out of her apartment. The cat had become a real annoyance, as it would pee and poop outside the litter box when she was out of town. She no longer wanted to deal with the cat and had come in to have it put down.

I was ready for this and did not hesitate. By this time, our cat, Missy, had already gone to her reward. After some discussion everybody agreed that I could take the cat. Our home would now have a cat again.

Bobby the Cat

The prior owner had told me the cat's name was Bubba—this was Texas, you understand. But we expatriates could not legitimately have a Bubba in our home, so we called it Bobby, a name that sounded close enough, so he would recognize it, hopefully. To avoid confusion with my wife's brother, whose name also is Bob, we dubbed our new family member Bobby the Cat.

Bobby the Cat, Gus, and Lacey in the Dallas sunshine

A little while later, we moved back up to Manhattan to live. I got everyone to New York in two trips. On one trip I took Bobby the Cat with me on a plane, with Bobby in a carrier on my lap. On the next trip, I drove Lacey, Gus, and Gigi from Dallas to New York City.

We were happy that the native Texas folks took well to the city.

Gus in particular seemed to take it in stride and in fact ate it all up. For instance, on his first walk on Manhattan's noisy and crowded Third Avenue near our apartment, he actually demanded that we stop so he could sit down and just watch all the traffic and people go by. Elaine took him on some of her shopping trips and remembers how he would strut about Macy's like he owned the place, the center of so much attention. We must have looked funny as I walked the three of them, so different—Lacey the sheltie, Gus the dachshund, and Gigi the toy poodle—through Central Park each morning.

You can tell a lot about people from how they react to the same thing. Once when I was flying for my job, I sat next to a lady, and we started talking about our pets. I was carrying a picture of Gus on me at the time, so I took it out and showed it to her.

When she saw it, she laughed heartily.

It wasn't a month later when I was on another flight and found myself sitting next to another lady who liked to chat. We got around to talking about our pets, and again I pulled out my picture of Gus.

She looked at it with a puzzled expression and said, "But that is the back of his head."

Oh, well.

Gigi later unexpectedly left us, rather early, at twelve years old, with a cancerous tumor in her stomach. Gus and Gigi had spent most of their years together, and Gus was affected by the loss.

"This is where they buried my friend Gigi."

Elaine wanted another black toy poodle to remind her of Gigi. The breeder we settled on showed us two puppies and asked us to choose between them. We took both.

The puppies, Vivian (more grayish) and Pamela (more blackish) were a wild, rambunctious twosome.

But old Gus and Bobby the Cat quickly took them in hand.

One of the things Gus was insistent on was that the puppies learn about their ancestors and show them respect. So he took them to where Gigi had been buried and explained the story of Gigi. At first they thought it was some kind of game, but he got them to understand, little by little.

Gus regularly visited Gigi's place by himself and would spend some quiet time with his old friend.

In time the little ones did grasp how to respect their ancestors. When they were grown up, they learned the pain of loss as Gus had.

"My name is Pammy."

"My name is Vivie."

The daughter of the lady homeowner on one side of our house wanted to have a dog for her infant son, so she spent $1,800 she could ill afford to get a "puggle," which is a combination beagle and pug. Pretty quickly it dawned on her that the dog was too big and rough for her infant, and she exiled the dog to the backyard.

There he would bark and howl most of the day and run away every other day, it seemed. The police would bring him back, and the whole neighborhood got to know this runaway, which she called Buddy. Being right next door, and with the separating fence being a low cyclone fence, I got to know

Buddy well. I would give him some water when it seemed there was none around their yard.

This went on for about eight months, until the day the young mother decided to move out with her husband. There seemed to be some ambiguity as to what would happen to Buddy. I asked, and I received. Buddy joined our household.

Buddy

The two toy poodles, Vivie and Pammy, were still around when we got Buddy, near the tail end of their lives. Buddy was as gentle as could be with them, and I even think that they took a big-sister liking to the new member of the house.

The next entry to our circle of pets, Lilly, was bittersweet. I inherited her from my beloved friend Nancy, who passed away from cancer last year.

Lilly

Buddy and Lilly already had known each other for several years and had stayed at each other's homes now and then. Lilly certainly greatly missed her mommy, but she fit in quickly at our house.

Finally, the lady neighbor on the other side of us approached me one day and begged me—we were close friends after many years as neighbors—to take a cat she had on her hands. The cat belonged to one of her sons. He was moving out of an apartment with his girlfriend, and the new place they were moving into did not allow pets. (Sound familiar?)

She herself already had three cats, and she said that her husband had threatened to move out if she acquired another. That was how we got our next cat, Bobby the Cat having left the earth a while earlier. Since my neighbor said that the cat was a handful and because of my first impressions of him, I decided that this ruffian needed a suitable name. He was named Paulie, after Paulie the limousine driver at Newark Airport.

Arthur J. Paone

Paulie

My friendly neighbor's explanation of why she wanted me to take the cat off her hands was thrown into doubt a month later. I listened in amazement to how she was fighting with the local ASPCA to adopt a cat that for some reason they just did not want her to have. She was petitioning their national headquarters, and so on. Eventually she won and got another cat to go along with her others. Now I wondered why she didn't want the one she had foisted off to me. I let it go and did not point out to her the obvious. We liked Paulie and had no reason to complain. But it was curious.

Paulie the cat does not share the socializing nature of our prior cats, Missy and Bobby the Cat. It has been years, but he still will try to whack Buddy whenever he comes within striking distance. He does not do that to the other dogs, though they all give him a wide berth.

It is not that Buddy is an innocent. Far from it. Take, for example, when the cat is trying to have a peaceful dinner. Who is staring at him? None other than our friend.

Then he often positions himself on a stairway or in front of the doggie door to prevent Buddy from coming down or up the stairs or going in or out of the house. Buddy will bark until one of us comes around to move Paulie.

On the other hand, he will often jump up on my lap to sit for a while and purr or lie on my stomach while I am reading in bed.

Sometimes Lilly seems to be a little concerned when Paulie gets too close to my face.

Each morning I take Buddy and Lilly to the beach, where we meet up with some dog friends for an hour's walk and then some coffee.

Most of my dog-walking friends are a little younger than I am, so I often find myself bringing up the rear. But I usually find my Lilly waiting for me.

On the other hand...

A wholly different but satisfying approach to sharing your life with lovable animals is to volunteer at a shelter. Get up each day and bring joy to yourself and a little dog or cat that is imprisoned in some cage. Take it out and walk it around. Hold it and say hello.

Visiting Nursing Homes Plan

If you are not in a nursing home in your eighties, you might want to bring some cheer to those who are. This is the only thing you can do, but it is a big one. Sadness permeates these homes, with angry, depressed, and unhappy souls who feel that their families and the world have abandoned them. A genuine smile from a stranger to briefly brighten their day is what you will be bringing them.

This is not for the faint of heart nor anyone who gets easily depressed. Today's nursing homes are pretty gruesome places. We haven't gotten around to making these places anywhere near acceptable for human beings, primarily because they are still for the most part for-profit businesses. The proprietors calculate down to the penny the amounts from Medicaid they can pocket after dispensing only what they absolutely have to in housing these unfortunates.

These homes are still dumping grounds where sad, lonely creatures are waiting for the end, attended to by low-paid workers who for the most part have little cultural or emotional sensitivity to the people they are supposedly taking care of. Profit is still the name of the game in this industry, and it shows in these places. The government has its regulations and its inspections, but the places seem as bleak today as they did thirty years ago.

There are nursing homes in every community. You can choose one nearby or visit a bunch within reach.

The beauty of this Plan is that just being yourself is all the equipment or expertise you need. Walking into the lobby of a nursing home and just saying hello will make the day for you and for the person you say hello to.

There is the risk of getting depressed by seeing these lonely people, some not entirely with us. But this risk can be alleviated if you also have a stiff drink before going in. Spread your cheer.

You can visit a different home each time or the same one, or even volunteer for one or more of them. You can make up a full schedule of just playing records for a room full of wandering and woe-begotten humans. Smiles will descend on you for the smallest favors—a wink, a hello, some music, a dog visit, whatever. It is easy work, except for the heavy cloud hanging over all these places.

This is a chancy program, but it offers the best opportunities for the rare happy moment. If you can feel happy about making just one of these inmates feel happy, even momentarily, then your day has been made—as has that of the inmate.

"Numbers Runner" Plan

The flourishing and ubiquitous numbers rackets of years ago have dwindled if not extinguished, thanks primarily to the government getting into the act. Well, government was always in the numbers rackets, but only in an unofficial way. Precinct captains protected them for payments, and so on. Today, lotteries and other legal betting games are so numerous and easy to play that it is not worthwhile for illegal gamblers to take the risk of competing. But there are still pockets of resistance where you might find some numbers games going on. Look for them and see if you can volunteer as a runner.

More exciting would be to set up a numbers game in your own neighborhood or town. Everyone is ready to gamble, particularly if it is a dollar for a number. If you cannot find a numbers game in your area, you could just set one up, giving yourself and a lot of fellow eighty-year-olds something interesting to do.

Each numbers game requires an organization with someone fixing the numbers and acting as the "bank." From the bank there would be "runners" who go back and forth between the individual bettors and the bank, transferring orally the bets and the payouts. Cash back and forth.

Eighty-year-olds would be great as runners, or walkers, or even walkers with walkers. They would not raise any suspicions as they visit individuals to take their bets or make payoffs. In return, the runner would be out and about, socializing with people and sharing the news.

In this system you would choose your own territory so that you can shape the job as you want—the area covered and the type of people you see. Perfect.

Bag Ladies Plan

I visualize for our eighty-year-olds a modified bag lady program, based on your particular likes and dislikes. For instance, ladies living near a beach can walk the beach with a bag and collect debris to clean up the beach. This would be good both for the beach and our bag lady. People in the city can pick up stuff on the sidewalk. It might be more difficult except in quiet neighborhoods.

Needless to say, both men and women can follow this Bag Ladies Plan.

Incidentally, be careful that you do not accumulate any of the stuff you collect. Then you might wander over into the hoarder category, a place you do not want to go. Collect the stuff and then get rid of it, even if you have to put it out as trash in front of your own home. But that probably will not be necessary, as in most communities there are enough public places to properly dispose of what you have collected.

I see enterprising old folks with shopping baskets full of plastic bottles they have collected. This involves a different type of collecting—for money. I am not recommending this, as the competition is unpleasant. When you bring your hoard to the deposit centers, you are treated like shit. That is not fun. My Plan for Bag Ladies is to make the world better by making it cleaner. You will feel a lot richer that the crummy change you could squeeze out of deposits. I hate to seem elitist, but we plan to have fun in our eighties, not stress.

The Bagmen Plan

An eighties-plus lady or gentleman shuffling into a congressman's office would raise little suspicion. They are already a regular fixture of legislative halls, threatening mayhem on anyone who touches their Medicare or Social Security. No one would dream that the old-timer was carrying an envelope stuffed with cash for the corrupt congressman.

Under this Plan, folks in their eighties would be the stealth couriers in our political system. With telephones, computers, and everything else now being monitored by the FBI, the CIA, the Russians, the Chinese, and maybe some guy on a couch somewhere, politicians and their masters are in dire need for ever more secret means of communication.

Hence, the parade of shuffling oldsters. They will be the stealth messengers of our entire political system. Demand will be high for anyone in his or her eighties who can still walk. Those who can also travel will be in even higher demand. I envision full employment for our generation.

There is no question that the American political system has been bought by people with money. There is no need to investigate details when a simple overview discloses the picture perfectly: tax laws written for the already rich, hugely wealthy citizens who pay little or no taxes while the rest of us are boxed tightly into inescapable scales of federal and local taxes; drug prices going higher; patent protection for the drug industry getting stronger while the path to cheaper generics gets more difficult; the rich getting richer and the poor getting poorer. This does not happen accidentally or by the laws of nature.

Much of the money greasing the wheels of **Government for the Rich** is "legal," in the form of political contributions to candidates and campaigns.

Few politicians would fail to follow the biddings of their Big Donors. But much of it is still technically "illegal," simple cash bribes to bypass what there are of laws and regulations that still get in the way. It is the latter that creates the opportunity for this Plan.

"Under the Table"

A large and varied group of entities have been feeding our politicians under the table, and there is no sign of this food frenzy slowing down. High on the list of employers for these stealth emissaries are the people pushing drugs, legal and illegal.

I hope that most of the eighty-year-olds who choose this Plan for their next ten years will decide to work for the legal drug pushers. It will be safer for them. But the illegal cartels would probably pay at a higher scale, so keep them in mind.

US deaths from drug overdoses (a government estimate is 71,073 people annually, or about 200 a day), and **prices** for essential medications have been increasing at rapid rates, a sign that both the illegal drug dealers and the legal drug dealers are having a heyday today in America.

Just today (November 1, 2018, All Saints Day), we were given another example of systemic corruption in our government.

In a move that flabbergasted critics, the FDA has approved an easy-to-administer, single-dose, under-the-tongue opioid that is **ten times as powerful as the highly addictive opioid fentanyl**.

"There is absolutely no need for this product," as one prominent scientist put it. The FDA chairman countered with the argument that it was needed for soldiers on the battlefield, ignoring that they already have more than enough opioids, including the fentanyl that many wounded veterans have found themselves addicted to after their service. The FDA chairman also promised that unlike other addictive drugs previously approved by the FDA, this time they intended really to control the dispensation of this one so as to prevent its abuse. Really?

When I was in the hospital for a busted appendix earlier this year, I was hallucinating just two days into a regime of painkillers. It's obvious that we already have more than enough painkillers out there. We don't need another "easily administered" opioid ten times as powerful as fentanyl. Yet while it is so obvious that this new drug application is not needed and could only present more danger to the public, why has the FDA approved it? It is hard not to conclude that the FDA is controlled by the drug industry.

Addiction deaths and high drug prices are two national plagues that are on parallel courses. As a result, there is a growing outcry across the country and at all levels of society for "something" to be done.

This clamor from the people that "something" needs to be done does not rattle the drug companies or the drug cartels. They have been there before. It simply means additional entries on the expense side of their ledgers, more cash to pour into the political system—that is, into the pockets of politicians, agency officials, and bureaucrats to stiffen their backbones. Luckily for us eighties-pluses, more and bigger cash payments to government officials will increase the need for us as couriers. Here's where we stealth couriers will come into our own. There will be work all around just from these two industries.

Of course, the legal and illegal drug people are not the only ones trying to influence politicians and government agencies, which ostensibly exist to protect us. The list of people trying to bypass the laws through cash payments is endless, at both the national and the local levels.

The job opportunities for a bagman start at the very local and neighborhood level, affording opportunities for seniors who find it difficult to travel to the state capital or to Washington, DC.

Do not doubt for a moment that there is any scarcity of corrupt politicians at all levels. There are two forms of corruption: the active and the passive.

There is the active form—the ones who pocket the cash. Then there is the passive form—colleagues on the city council or legislative body, other employees in an agency, who know that someone is taking cash under the table but turn a blind eye to it.

I suppose there are several rational explanations why this phenomenon exists—evil in a blatantly open display that no one seems to see. But in political corruption, I think the dominant reason is that all the people in the Turn a Blind Eye Crowd have their own games going and do not want to rock the boat. They don't want any bright lights shining into their chambers that might discover relatives on the payroll who don't belong there, second or third government pensions that are drowning the taxpayers, dubious side jobs that would not look good, connections with people that may raise questions, favors already received or expected from the person pocketing the cash in front of their eyes.

We were treated to some fun textbook examples of political corruption about a dozen years ago in New Jersey when then US attorney Chris Christie sent a parade of small-time politicians (mostly from the *other* party and nobody powerful) across the front pages and into jails for short-term stints.

In addition to newspaper accounts, I have used as my source for this fun episode a well-written book by two reporters, Ted Sherman and Josh Margolin, The Jersey Sting: A True Story of Crooked Pols. New York: St. Martin's Press, 2011.

When Chris Christie was a young and impatiently ambitious US attorney in New Jersey in 2002, he wanted to make a name for himself—a fighter against public corruption. There is a distinction between making a name for oneself as a fighter against corruption and actually eliminating corruption. He didn't want to rock the boat too much and was not about to risk taking on anyone really important, particularly any of his political friends. What he did instead was just pick the lower-hanging fruit in the other party's orchards, as a friend of mine once described it.

The federals had caught a bizarrely audacious New Jersey small-time real estate developer for passing a bad check in the astounding amount of $25 million. With little prodding, he agreed to be an informant. He was wired up and sent out to compromise as many Democratic local officeholders as possible by offering small bribes in return for promises of petty favors such as zoning variances, accelerated planning board hearings, and the like. He showed the same insanely audacious spirit in pursuing his prey that he showed in passing multimillion-dollar checks on accounts that had zero balances.

He found that any politician with functioning hands quickly grabbed the money. It was like taking candy from a baby—or, rather, giving candy to a baby. Rarely did a mayor or member of the local council turn down the bribe. The only ones who did were the more sophisticated crooks whose long experience in corruption gave them a sixth sense for spotting an informant. Christie made headline after headline with his busts—a whole lot of small fries were enough to make him a big dog, the governor of New Jersey.

Things are not much better today and perhaps are even worse. For example, as I am writing this, it is just a few weeks to the November 6, 2018, elections, at which my choice for US senator in New Jersey will be between a criminal and a drug lord.

Please do not think for a moment that I am picking on New Jersey. It is just that I am more familiar with New Jersey. A brief glance at other states would show the same pernicious corruption deep in their political systems.

In New York, for example, they finally put away the Speaker of the Assembly, who for decades was milking the system while his colleagues, who were being taken care of in other ways by him and whatever governor was presiding at the time, played their "turn a blind eye" roles. This happened just after the leader of the State Senate, from the other political party, had also been sent to jail. Then, soon thereafter, a bunch of the governor's cronies "disappointed" him and also found themselves going to jail for one form of corruption or other.

Do we need to discuss the politics of Alabama or Mississippi, or Illinois or Florida, or Wyoming or Nevada, just name a few states? I could go on but won't. I am sure you get the idea. We are not a banana republic yet, but we are getting there.

Then there is the "Common Sense" Test.

Instead of trying to prove that our political system is corrupt by showing how politicians have been caught red handed with their hands in the till, let's take a look at our political system from another perspective. Let us ask the simple, common-sense question: Why do we always get the short end of the stick?

Ask ourselves: If we are living in a democracy where the will of the people should be reflected in our laws and policies, why are there so many laws and policies that are against the overwhelming majority of Americans? Why are the rich always getting richer and the poor getting poorer?

Almost every politician always says the right thing and promises us everything we want when we elect her or him to office. But once they are there, they become part of the rich man's system. Or they just set up shop for the enrichment of themselves and their relatives.

No matter whom we send to Washington or the state capital to fight for us, in the end we always find ourselves on the bottom. The rich get richer and the poor get poorer. Why is that? How did we miss that sleight of hand? That con job? We didn't even see it when it happened, but it happened.

This little book of fluff is not the place to try to explain how that happens, nor am I capable of doing that for you. How the rich get their will done, at our expense, would require an analysis of many areas of influence in this country. Just one aspect is that so many people vote contrary to their own interests—having traded their sacred franchise in return for their **Single Issue**. The Single-Issue Voter. If you are for THIS or against THAT, then I don't care what the hell else you do, even if you grind me down even more.

Thus, if the scoundrel is against abortion, I don't care what he does about tax cuts for the rich, deregulation that dirties our air and water but helps big corporations, or the undermining of labor unions, which hurts the workers but enriches the already rich. If he is against giving free things to the ignorant and lazy poor, then he can give himself as many tax breaks as he wants. And so on.

It can get awfully complicated, and I won't go there right now. I will stick with the question of proving that our political system is corrupt by asking some common-sense questions.

We call ourselves a democracy, and in a democracy, the government is supposed to reflect **our** interests. So we have to ask questions when we find that so many policies enacted and enforced by OUR government are mysteriously **against** the will of the people.

My explanation for this "mystery" is political corruption.

Let's take a look at just three issues to prove this conclusion: (1) The law that says the federal agency running Medicare cannot negotiate with drug companies for the prices it pays for drugs, (2) universal health care, and (3) assault weapons.

The Medicare "No Negotiation" Mandate

In 2003, when Congress authorized Medicare to pay for drugs, a good thing for both drug companies and senior citizens, it inserted into the law a curious provision, this one good only for the drug companies. Section 1395w-111(i) of 42 USC reads as follows:

> *In order to promote competition under this part and in carrying out this part, the Secretary-*
> 1. *may not interfere with the negotiations between drug manufacturers and pharmacies and PDP [prescription drug plans] sponsors; and*
> 2. *may not require a particular formulary or institute a price structure for the reimbursement of covered part D drugs.*

This is the famous mandate that ensures "competition," and big profits, for the drug companies by prohibiting competition.

It ties the hands of the biggest purchaser of drugs in the United States, Medicare, and allows the drug companies to charge Medicare whatever they want with no resistance from Medicare.

The provision in question affects what is called Part D of Medicare. Under Part D, Medicare in 2016 paid out to the drug companies about $106 billion for forty-three million people. That $106 billion represents about 30 percent of all drug costs in the United States for that year.

You might say that it does not make common sense to prohibit one side of a supposedly free-market purchase from being able to negotiate. It seems to me, and to most Americans, that you would be right. Yet that is what our government mandates. Polls show that eight out of ten Americans believe that Medicare should be able to negotiate drug prices with the drug companies. Nevertheless, numerous attempts since 2003 in Congress to eliminate that "no negotiation" mandate have failed.

Why is this? What accounts for this "mystery"—our Congress repeatedly voting down something demanded by over 80 percent of the people?

What is it that encourages our representatives to so blatantly defy our wishes?

The answer begins with the flow of *legal* money.

In 2016 the two drug trade associations spent $152 million to lobby Congress while its members disbursed $20 million in direct political contributions. Nine out of ten House members and ninety-seven of one hundred senators received contributions from drug companies, with the leaders and committee chairman raking in the largest amounts.

Then there is the unknown flow of *illegal* money into Congress. The amount of this under-the-table, stuffed-envelope cash is unknown.

Mystery Number One—solved.

Universal Health Care

We are the richest nation on earth, yet millions of our citizens are without health care. Why is that?

What is UHC?

UHC means that all individuals and communities receive the health services they need without suffering financial hardship. It includes the full spectrum of essential, quality health services, from health promotion to prevention, treatment, rehabilitation, and palliative care.

UHC enables everyone to access the services that address the most important causes of disease and death, and ensures that the quality of those services is good enough to improve the health of the people who receive them.

This is the language used on the World Health Organization's website to define universal health care. It is very general and without details so that each country can fashion its own system.

Another definition of universal health care is given by a health advocate named Trisha Torrey:

"Universal health care" or "universal coverage" refers to a system of allocating health care resources where everyone is covered for basic health care services and no one is denied care as long as he or she remains legal residents in the territory covered—such as all the residents of the Commonwealth of Massachusetts, or all the citizens of the country of Canada.

It does not mean FREE health care for all. That would be financially impossible for most nations. Each country needs to figure out who pays for what, so long as everyone gets the health-care services they need and so long as it does not drive them into poverty.

It is not that we in the United States do not spend enough money on health care. We spend more per capita than any other country in the world, an annual amount of $3 trillion in 2017, or one-sixth of the country's economy—yet it is estimated that over 10 percent of the population is without medical insurance coverage.

The vast majority of Americans want universal health care—everyone should be able to get the health services they need. But there is less agreement on how to pay for it, and that is what the anti-UHC forces use to drive wedges between us. So we wind up with what they want us to have: a bloated, duplicative, heavily administered and expensive health-care system that still fails to reach all Americans but enriches various segments of the health-care industry.

I searched on Google for a list of countries with universal health care. I discovered that except for us, the developed world seems to be able to give all its citizens health care in one form or another. This should be embarrassing to us. Even worse, take a look at some of the dates when these countries started with universal health care. Some go back to the forties, when Europe was still in a devasted post–World War II condition. Here is one list from the New York State Department of Health's website:

Country	Start Date of Universal Health Care
Australia	1975
Austria	1967
Bahrain	1957
Belgium	1945
Brunei	1958
Canada	1966
Cyprus	1980
Denmark	1973
Finland	1972
France	1974
Germany	1941
Greece	1983
Hong Kong	1993
Iceland	1990
Ireland	1977
Israel	1995
Italy	1978
Japan	1938
Kuwait	1950
Luxembourg	1973
Netherlands	1966
New Zealand	1938
Norway	1912
Portugal	1979
Singapore	1993
Slovenia	1972
South Korea	1988
Spain	1986
Sweden	1955
Switzerland	1994
United Arab Emirates	1971
United Kingdom	1948

Now we have to ask the question: If every other developed country can come up with some kind of universal health care for its citizens, why can't we?

Assault Weapons

Nice, pretty girls do it.

Tough-looking ladies do it.

And of course, your average rugged-looking man does it.

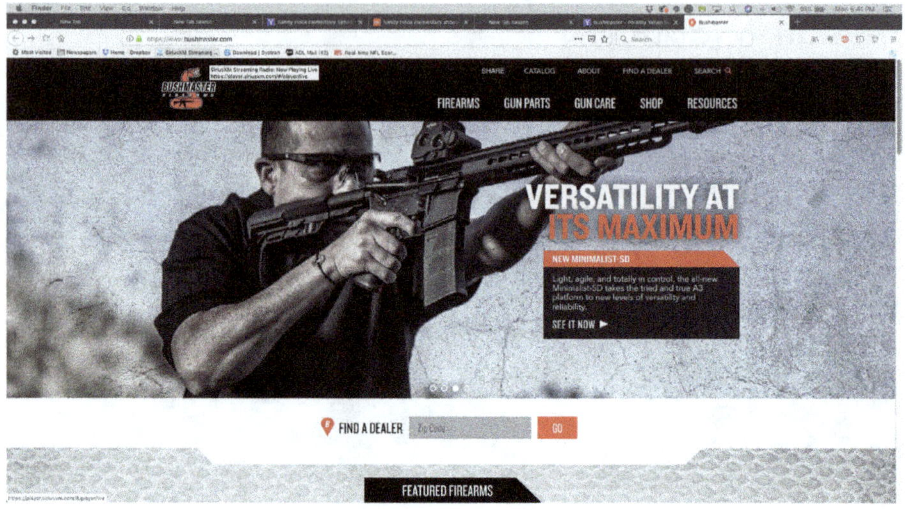

A couple of Saturdays ago, on October 27, 2018, a gunman killed eleven mostly elderly worshippers at the Tree of Life Synagogue in Pittsburgh. He used an AR-15 assault rifle and three Glock .357 handguns.

Assault rifles were used in February 2018 at the high school in Parkland, Florida, where seventeen were killed; at the Las Vegas massacre in October 2017, where fifty-nine were killed and five hundred wounded; at Orlando's Pulse nightclub in June 2016, where forty-nine were killed and dozens wounded; in San Bernardino, where fourteen people were killed in December 2015; and at Sandy Hook Elementary School, where twenty-seven were killed in December 2012.

These guns are available everywhere, with magazines holding up to thirty rounds.

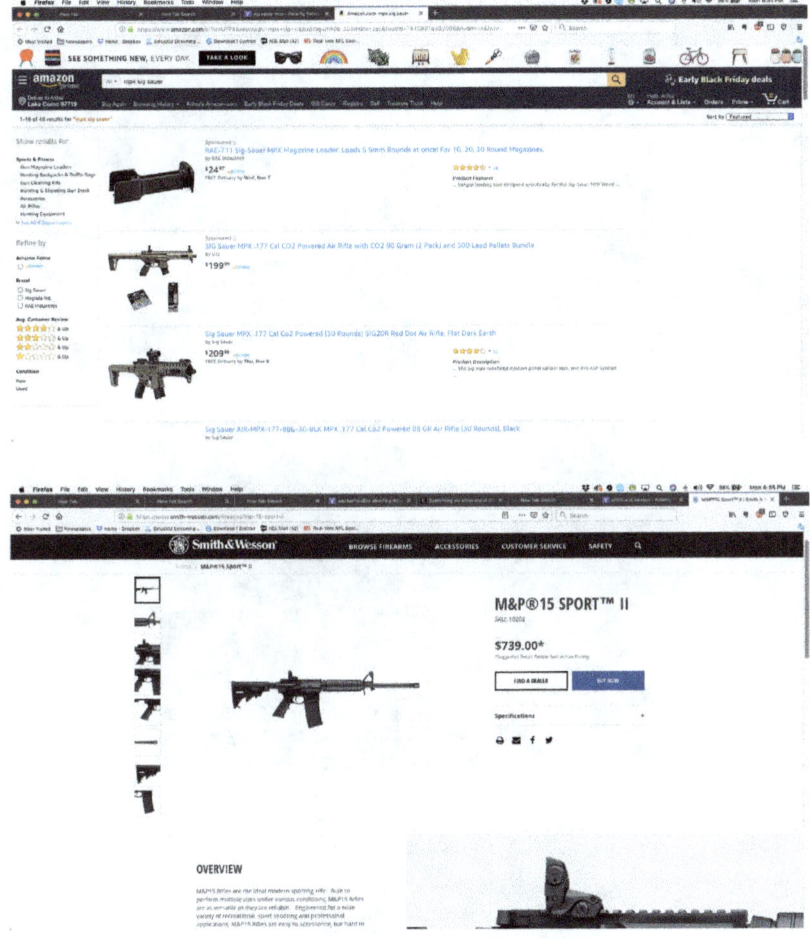

I know there are good people who have a passion for playing with military-style weapons.

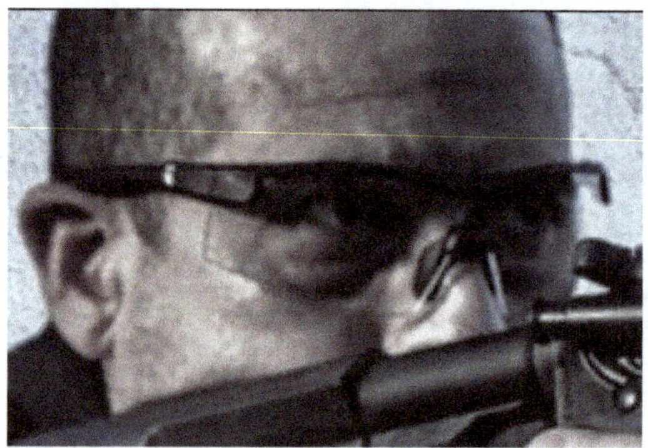

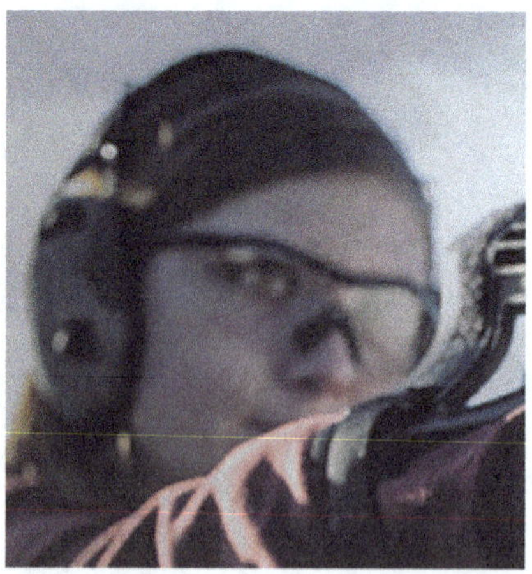

But please give the rest of us a break!

Again, the majority of Americans want a ban on assault weapons and high-capacity magazines. While a "sportsman" or "sportswoman" may get his or her jollies by pulverizing a target with thirty rounds of bullets a second, or whatever, the rest of us would like to keep them out of the hands of people killers.

All the killers in the mass shootings listed above bought their assault weapons LEGALLY. The rest of us would like a fighting chance. But Congress keeps rejecting efforts to ban assault weapons. For a short period, we did have a federal law banning assault weapons—and mass shootings went down. But after that temporary ban expired, all efforts to revive it have failed.

Why has Congress defied the will of the people?

At this point, you can answer that question.

Problem Number Three—solved.

One wanting to become a bagman should try to look disheveled and shuffle when moving about, which should not be hard for many of us to do without any practice. The prospective stealth carrier can canvass the local city council or go to the federal building and visit the congressman and offer his or her services. Since income would not be the object, but entertainment and activity, the bagman can offer a discount from the fee charged by the regular bagmen. In addition, the politician getting the payoffs will feel more comfortable that his bagmen will soon forget from whom he or she has picked up a bribe or paid it to.

Again, both men and women can become part of this Bagman Plan.

The Painting Plan

What do Dwight Eisenhower and Tony Bennett have in common? The same thing as George W. Bush and Winston Churchill.

They all took up painting as a hobby and got to be really good at it. Your Painting Plan could also include drawing and sculpture, though sculpture is a bit more difficult to get your arms around. With sculpture there is a need for larger space; materials that may be heavy, and so on. It's somewhat physical, but it will depend on what material you use. Certainly, sculpting in marble is a bit more strenuous than molding clay.

You should start by finding an art class at a community college. See what it takes to paint—what kind of materials you will need and how you go about starting a painting. Learn the ABCs at the community college and then set yourself up.

It will be fun to structure a place in your home as a studio. If you have to, you could even make a space in one of your rooms in an apartment for your "art studio."

One of our friends has set up a little studio in his garage and has produced some pretty impressive watercolors. None of us believed he really painted the stuff he showed us, so we visited the garage. It was true!

CARPE
DIEM
WELCOME
TO
BEACH HAVEN
SAIL MORE
WORRY LESS

One of Dave's paintings.

Forget about whether you have artistic talent. If you want to paint, you will ultimately be good at it. Someone once said that you can become an expert at anything if you spend ten thousand hours at it. I don't know if that is true, nor do I care. Nor should you. You are not painting for an exhibition; you will be painting for the joy of creation.

The Sports Plan

There is no reason why our eighty-plus crowd cannot engage in sports and make that a program. Two that come to mine are bird-watching and fishing.

Bird-Watching

If you have a backyard, you have all you need to establish a bird-watching regimen. First you will need to get two or three bird feeders, as birds will not come to your yard with any regularity unless there is some reason to. Birds are not to be underestimated. They also are in it for what they can get, like everybody else.

This picture is of my own backyard a few days ago (November 1, 2018). It took a while, perhaps a few years, to finally get the feeders in just the right configuration and location.

The birds seem to love it, as I have a flock of them every day, and they are a beauty to watch as they jump from feeder to branch to pole to feed, often in competition with one another.

The squirrels add another dimension as they play among themselves and the birds in the seed-droppings field.

The labels on bird food packages promise all sorts of wonders that their particular seeds can produce in attracting the rarest and most beautiful birds. Those labels are no different from the labels on the items in our grocery and health-food stores—they are for the birds. What you need to do is try one kind of seed and see what happens. Then try another, and so on. At one point, if you think a particular birdseed product works best, just stick with it. One consideration that I suggest you keep in mind is the amount of debris that any particular birdseed leaves on the ground. For instance, though sunflower seeds are very popular, the birds leave behind a lot of the seed shells. Some seeds do not have shells. That is just one item to put into your calculations. As for price, get the cheapest you can get. The prices for the basic seed packages are pretty competitive. There is absolutely no need to pay premium prices for birdseed, as the birds will not notice the difference.

If you are setting up bird feeders in your yard, please also put out one or more birdbaths for water. The birds do need water. Of course, while the squirrels are not allowed to share the feeders, they are welcome to the water.

Each day you need to put fresh water into the birdbaths and also check the contents of the bird feeders. There is nothing worse than sending word to the bird world that your yard is a comfort zone, only for them to find it a dried-up and empty desert. Keep everything clean and fully supplied with seeds and water.

Then you can sit back and watch the birds. They will come and play, chirp, sing, eat, and drink. A total delight. Some will chase one another, and others will sit in the most fascinating way on posts and fences and roofs. Every day will be different.

If you want to be sophisticated in your watching and get to know the names of the birds, you can go buy a book or two on birds. Usually the local book store will have a book about what birds are common in your area. In addition to a book on the local birds, you might also think about investing in the bible of bird-watching books: *The Sibley Guide to Bird Life and Behavior* by D. A. Sibley, C. Elphick, and J. B. Dunning (2001).

It should be enough just watching the birds and their friends the squirrels, who will also be attracted to cavort in your yard. But some bird-watchers go further and keep a keen eye out for rare birds. This will take some study on your part. The Sibley book will help identify rare birds. There are societies you can join and compare sightings, and so on. But it is up to you as to how deep you want to get.

Those who do not have yards or want to go beyond their yards can take to the public parks or the streams or rivers nearby. To avoid being mistaken for just another old person hanging around, make sure you obtain an interesting walking stick and, most importantly, a pair of binoculars. Some folks have dressed themselves in fancy bird-watching outfits, but you don't have to go that far. It will be enough to declare your intentions in public if you have a pair of binoculars hanging around your neck. It will help if the strap is odd looking, like a funny color. You don't want people thinking you are just peeping about. You need to play the role of bird-watching. Don't forget to stop periodically and point the binoculars into the air or toward a tree. You might actually see some birds.

Fishing

Fishing is just as easy to get into and at any level you wish.

I am most familiar with surf fishing, as I have always lived near the Atlantic Ocean, the last twenty years in a beach community. The little that I have learned about surf fishing is from observing the people who fish along the beach when I walk my dogs in the morning. They are a lucky bunch—out in the surf with the beautiful sky in millions of different formations.

You get the fella who is sitting on a timber pile that for some reason is sticking out of the sand at the right height with a rod in his hand. He is dressed just like me, for whatever the weather may be. Then another fisherman has a chair and a bucket and maybe a cap you could call a fisherman's cap. Still another seems to have walked out of an Orvis catalogue, dressed as your hobby fisherman from head to toe, with fancy rods—more than one—and distinguished-looking tackle boxes with expanding shelves displaying an admirable multitude of hooks, lures, rigs, sinkers, and other fishing gear. Just along a single beach, there seems to be a very wide latitude both in expertise and equipment.

Most of the people I see fishing along the shore seem to be men, though I guess a woman could do it as well. Sometimes I see a couple. I am told that in our area, the fishermen are catching striped bass when they are running during the year, and fluke in the summer. For the most part, if the catch is healthy and large enough, they take them home to cook and eat or give to their friends. A very few here just catch and release, fishing just for the fun of it. But that practice is more prevalent in other areas.

You should be able to find your own level of comfort in just a few tries.

Those of us who are near lakes and cities can find a pier and just drop a line into the water. Fortunately, our waters are cleaner today, and we can fish in more areas. I have read that, for instance, the piers along the Hudson even in Manhattan can be fished from.

I would not think boats are good for us, whether small ones or those big fishing boats with crowds of people along the rails. A little too much heavy lifting and tossing about.

You can get an inexpensive fishing reel and rod just about anywhere. While you can't fish very successfully in your yard, in most communities you can get to a beach or bay or river. With waters being cleaner today, a lot of places that were once hopeless for fishing have come back.

If you get more interested in fishing, you could visit a sports store and upgrade to more serious fishing stuff. Or you can stay at the single-rod level as long as you wish.

The "Moving Out, Moving In" Plan

This plan requires that you have extra money and some energy. It takes a lot of time and planning to organize a move, especially if you have been settled in your home for a good period of time.

But putting a place behind you and finding a new place could be an occupation in itself, especially at our age. All the heaving lifting, of course, will have to be done by hired help, and maybe you can delegate even the chore of deciding what to throw out in the move. It will even make it easier for the person who takes care of your affairs later—the less the better. But I can envision the excitement and wonder of looking for a new place. There would be so many things to test and explore before making a decision. It may call for travel, temporary stays, financial calculations—but what the hell. As they say, you live only once.

The "Coming Out" Plan

I am truly ambivalent whether an eighty-plus person who has spent a lifetime viewed as one gender should suddenly tell everyone that he or she was born the other gender.

I am forced to use the common terminology crafted somewhere along the way to discuss this topic. But I don't like terms such as "closet" and "coming out." They are infused with implications, and I think they were created by someone who was trying to prejudge a complex situation and frame it too simply, perhaps reflecting his or her own personal situation.

One who is gay or lesbian and chooses not to identify with that category should not be considered to be in a "closet." It assumes darkness, fear, shame, hiding, and so on. They themselves may consider they situation quite differently, and we should not be assuming that they are in hiding and just dying to escape something or other.

However, this philosophical analysis is beyond me and this book of fluff. I want to concentrate on whether an eighty-year-old who has lived one way his or her entire life should now announce a different sexual preference.

I have to ask: What's the point? Is it worth it?

None of us live in a vacuum. We have relatives, friends, neighbors. What we do affects others, for better or worse.

We need to ask: Is it worth the trouble at this point?

If we have not already come out at this stage, we must be pretty adjusted to living that way, rather than the way we were born. Do we really have time to readjust? Do we want to subject our friends and relatives to the shock? And for what?

It seems to me that to do this at eighty-plus, one would have to have some really powerful motivation. I can visualize such motivation.

But it is highly unlikely that we will get the motivation like that former Cowboys linebacker from the eighties had who came out a few days ago, November 14, 2018, by way of a same-sex wedding announcement—a cute little thing sitting on our lap or clinging to us. If anybody looking like that pays any attention to you, it must be because you have some money, and you better remember the old adage: "There is no fool like an old fool."

Photo by Allen Zaki

I doubt it would have been a newsworthy event for the *New York Times* if the fifty-nine-year-old former linebacker had just announced that he was getting married again. He had divorced about ten years earlier, and his two teenage children were living with him. What attracted so much attention to the announcement, however, was that he was marrying another and much younger guy. The broadcast was so unexpected to some of his friends that one of them actually returned the wedding invitation with a comment about what a good joke it was.

You need to keep in mind that if you have not come out of the closet by the time you are eighty, you can expect even more of that kind of reaction from some of your friends and relatives. It is OK for a fifty-nine-year-old guy to say "The hell with it. I'm going to do what I've always wanted to do." But it is different for an eighty-year-old gal or guy.

On the other hand, it is true that the times have changed, and our coming out will not cause us to be ostracized. I have not checked, but I must assume that by this time most adult communities and assisted-living facilities have no difficulty with same-sex couples. I have not heard of any of them as being predominately same-sex venues, but that may come as we move along.

The Staying-Healthy Plan

If you are reading this at eighty or eighty-plus and are relatively healthy, then your Ten-Year Plan is to just keep doing what you're doing.

If you are reading this at eighty or eighty-plus and your health is poor, well, what can I say? Good luck and hang in there!

In truth, you had better be getting some exercise or your body will stiffen up and every move will become harder. Stretch your limbs, stretch them every day and often, again and again.

There are some exercises I would not recommend, definitely not recommend, things like this —

If you can afford it, try joining a gym of some sort. Find one that accommodates older people and where you feel comfortable. Don't be afraid to try out their free trial periods. You need to be comfortable, or you won't go there on a regular basis, as you should.

I myself keep trying to find a regular "exercise" thing to do, such as a gym or stationary bike riding at home. But so far, my only regular exercise is walking my dogs on the beach each morning for about an hour. It's probably not good enough, but it will do for now, until I work myself into something else.

Doing Things around the House Plan

This is something that takes up a lot of my own time and gives me a feeling of satisfaction. There's nothing like "Ah. Finally got it done!"

If you own a house, this is possibly for you. There are some prerequisites. You have to be a little, but not very, handy; have a spouse—if you have one—who is not afraid to have you pick up a hammer and do the job rather than insisting on calling "the man"; be comfortable with a fungible interpretation of local code regulations and permit requirements ("It's my house! The hell with them!"); and be willing to make mistakes: blow out fuses, get cuts, screw up the coloring, drop a two-by-four on your foot, and get a little temporary flooding once in a while, not to mention "lights out" episodes.

If you can put that under your belt or apron, then you can do anything. With Home Depot, Lowe's, and YouTube, the world of home improvement is limited only by your imagination and your budget.

My father and his father were tailors, and I was a lawyer when I worked for a living. So there was nothing about wood, tools, bricks, and construction in my bloodline or training. But along the way, I just picked up things. You can do the same thing.

I think it started when my wife, Elaine, and I bought our first house in Dallas. Back then, in 1980, there was no YouTube, and I don't think any Home Depot. But I did some tile work and odds and ends in the backyard and around the house. Nothing too significant, but it was a beginning for a weekend home improver.

My home improvements took off years later in Belmar when we got a house for weekends that turned out to be our retirement house. Elaine's father was still alive, and he was a vast source of information and expertise on home projects—he knew everything in plumbing and electricity. His father was an electrician. I leaned on him often for advice.

Soon I will take you through some of the projects I did in this house that I can remember and still have some pictures of. It may give you some inspiration and ideas.

At the time we also had an apartment in Manhattan on East Seventieth Street near Second Avenue. I was extremely lucky to have latched on to a first-floor apartment in a brownstone with a private backyard—tiny but still a backyard and our own—and a good-natured landlord who welcomed pets. A rarity, but it happens.

Here I started my life of home projects with the most compelling—a ramp for my dogs to get down into the yard. The first floor was actually a stairway distance up from the ground level, so to get the dogs down into the backyard, I needed a ramp. The metal steps that were in place were much too steep for them to handle.

This was Manhattan, and it was not easy to transport lumber and such around. But somehow I got three giant planks of outdoor wood into the apartment and set up the ramp from our back door. It was wonderful.

The only picture I have of that is just a glimpse of Lacey in the doorway at the top of the ramp. It worked perfectly for us for the seven or eight years or so we were there.

At the same time, back down in our weekend place in Belmar, we had the same compelling issue: how to set things up so that the dogs and cat could come in and out of the backyard at their pleasure. Now remember, I had only the weekends and evenings to operate, as I was still working. I was really hustling.

The first thing I did was punch a hole into the wall under the window facing the backyard. That would serve as the doggie door.

Then it was easy to lay down some planks of wood to serve as a ramp. That was it for a while, and it served the purpose.

This served us well for a while. Bobby the Cat, Lacey, Gus, and Gigi got used to it very quickly.

Then it occurred to us that we would like to go out to the backyard in the same say that the animals did. Otherwise, we had to go over to the side of the house and walk around to the back. Thus, the next project was to evolve the doggie door into the people-and-doggie door.

I removed the windows, enlarged the opening, and installed some sliding doors. Not a big deal, and it looked great.

But now we had to have a much more substantial platform and stairs for people. A little trickier. I enlisted my brother-in-law Bob for assistance.

Now that I had replaced the doggie door with regular sliding doors, we had to replace the small platform at the top of the doggie ramp.

First, we had to get some piles up to support a strong platform.

Then some measuring for stairs. We got the wood, outdoor stair frames, and steps from Home Depot. At that time there was no Lowe's store around us.

Everybody was helping out.

Before long, there it was!

In the interest of full disclosure, I have to confess that it was not long after completion of the new ramp and stairs that I killed that beautiful cherry-blossom tree you see in the foreground. I had gotten it into my head that I wanted to clean the brick patio area next to the dog ramp. Either I had read somewhere, or someone had told me, that you can clean brick with acid. So that was what I did. The tree died soon thereafter. Of course, the acid got under the bricks where the roots of the tree must have run.

Lesson: you learn from your mistakes.

The house in Belmar we purchased was at first used just as a weekend place by the beach. I retired and spent most of my time there while Elaine continued working in New York City. Eventually she closed the place in New York City and now works out of the house.

It was built, along with a mirror house across the common driveway, by a pair of brothers-in-law. Both were World War II veterans and were familiar with construction; I believe one or both of them ran or owned a hardware store. It was a sturdy one-family house and not just a beach cottage, but they added on to it over the years. First they added a dormer upstairs and then an extension, which is now our TV room and part of the kitchen. So the house is already pretty much a mix and match when it comes to electrical wiring and plumbing.

A couple of years after we bought it, some friends came to visit, Carmen and Celia. I have been trying to find a photo I took of Carmen sitting in the living room, which would show you where my next project was. But I just cannot find the picture.

I have sketched an outline for you to see what I am talking about. In the illustration I am sitting with my back to you and facing Carmen and the side of the house I want to speak about. You will notice behind him, to our right, is the front door to the house. The only other opening is that small window over Carmen's shoulder.

I found that this opening to the world was just much too small. There had to be a much larger view of what was happening out there. I got to work.

I measured out what I thought would be a nice big front window. Then I went to Home Depot to find something. Getting a window that size was a big and complicated, not to say expensive, custom-made order. So I looked around the store. I settled on utilizing the stationary part of a two-part set of patio doors. One door was stationary, and the other one in the set moved. To fit my space, I needed three of the stationary doors, which would act as my front window.

I wasn't sure the store would let me take the sets apart, but they did. I left with three patio doors, the stationary halves of three sets.

Now came the fun. I sawed and hammered out the wall to create the opening I needed, careful to set up some supports to make sure the roof wouldn't cave in while I was at it. While I was carrying a large section of the removed wall to the back of the house, a lady neighbor I had not met yet from down the block gave me the thumbs-up as she rode by on her bicycle.

These were the days when Elaine was still in New York City for the week and also traveling a lot. Consequently, I was able to get most of the job done before she came home to see it. That was the only way I could even start a project like this, as she would have screamed "No, no!" if she had known what I was doing.

Fortunately, we had been in the house only a little while; hence, neither of us had set any roots yet. In addition, she was very busy with her work, so the house was not a big thing in her life. But still, she would have said no.

Most of my projects were done that way, and she always liked how they ended up. There were complaints about timing and running into the holidays, and some complaints about expenses, but all in all, she accepted things and was even pleased with most of the jobs I did.

Back to my chopping a big hole in the front of the house. The dogs had a lot of fun going in and out of the new opening.

The view from the inside was like being in a different house.

Everybody just loved the finished product.

In our backyard, when we bought the house, we had two pretty old sheds. One was used by the former owner as a workshop. He even had one wall lined with drawers that had different screws, nuts, and other fasteners in them; a large worktable; a dozen electric sockets; lights; and a coal-burning stove. He certainly knew what he was doing. Must have done some neat work out there.

The other shed was used for storage—garden tools and the like. This one seemed to be in a greater state of decay.

At one point I decided to redo the scene. I wanted to change the workroom shed into a livable space, a little cottage where I could read and listen to music.

The other old storage shed I wanted to replace with a nice, new one to store garden tools, lawn mower, snow blower, and so on.

Shed on the left to be converted to a "cottage" and the one on the right to be removed and replaced by new storage shed.

Initially, I tried to do things like everybody else. It was a big job, and I wasn't looking for trouble. I would stay, like a reasonable person, within my limits.

I got on the internet and used one of those ubiquitous service listings to find a local contractor. When he came, I explained what I wanted to do with the work shed—gut it and put in some nice wood walls and floor, a lot of windows, and a heating unit of some sort.

He promptly went down to the municipal offices and presumably asked them what the local code and permit requirements were for my prospective job.

A Boy Scout!

OK, I am generally comfortable with that concept. We should all try to comply with electrical, plumbing, building, etc. code requirements, as they exist for our benefit and safety. But in some cases, they do not make any sense, and this was one of them.

According to my contractor, the code officer said that we could not just gut the shed and renovate it. Instead, we had to take out the old cement foundation and put in a new one. This seemed extreme, but I was willing to consider that this requirement was within the realm of reason.

But then my contractor came up with the killer: to construct the new foundation, we first had to dig the entire space down four feet deep, just as if we were building a house!

There definitely was something wrong here. I said goodbye to the contractor. Curiously, he seemed not to mind that at all. Now I suspected that he just did not want this small but complicated job in the first place, and he had set out to make it seem impossible. Of course, the internet listing on which I found him claimed that all the contractors advertised were willing to do any job, big or small. I guess not.

Well, in the spirit of one door closing and another door opening, I got down to work.

Acting as my own contractor, I hired a garbage guy to gut the cottage shed and demolish the storage shed. It was fun watching that stuff go down.

The shed that I was going to convert to my little cottage was in bad shape.

Eventually, the shed that was to be my cottage got gutted, and I had a clean slate to work with.

The storage shed, on the other hand, disappeared entirely.

To replace the storage shed, I found a do-it-yourself supplier online. When it was delivered, the hundred or so pieces of wood took up most of our driveway. Each piece of wood had a letter on it, and eventually, with the help of a little booklet they included and a friend or two, I put it together.

For my cottage-to-be, I had a wood frame shell with a roof and concrete floor to work with. I bought the best hardwood for the floor and good wood—I think pine—for the walls from Lowe's or Home Depot. The guy selling me the stuff warned me that the wood would warp in an outdoor small building unless I keep the temperature moderate and the moisture low. I assured him that the building would be properly insulated, heated in the winter, and cooled in the summer. So I made sure that there was enough insulation in the walls and the ceiling. I put in an air conditioner and a ceiling fan. And a gas-burning stove for heat.

I had a problem with the ceiling fan I installed, as the blades kept hitting the ceiling or the beams. It took me a while to cut the blades to the right size, but I still do not trust it and never put that fan on.

The first air conditioner I bought, maybe about $300, did not work at all. It required 220 electricity, which I did not have in the cottage. Since I had installed it and banged it up quite a bit in the process, I could not return it to the store. To disguise it so Elaine would not realize that I was throwing it out, I disassembled it and put the pieces out for garbage pickup a few at a time. My plan didn't work, as I later learned that she had noticed it. I got an air conditioner that worked.

The only other item that set me back for a while was the gas stove. The store I bought it from, paying something over $3,000, refused to help me install it unless I got all the local permits. I was pretty sure this meant running the gas line three or four feet under the yard from the house, and that would have been a nuisance and prohibitively expensive. I was not afraid of installing it myself, but I would need help making the gas connections, as that did give me some pause.

I researched it all on the internet—with Google and YouTube, you can find out how to do anything. An outside line for gas running aboveground was perfectly OK. For a few hundred dollars, I bought a flexible outdoor gas line and ran it along the fence from the basement to the gas stove in the cottage. A friend's son was an apprentice plumber, and he helped me with the gas connections.

I got some great-big picture windows and only the best cedar shingles for the roof and walls. For nails I learned that you had to be careful. Not only were we outdoors, but the shingles splintered easily and needed special stainless-steel nails. The local places did not carry the grade that the internet said was best—telling me something about the local contractors who installed them—so I ordered the nails from a nail manufacturer. Of course, I bought fifty times more than I needed and have the surplus hidden away in the storage shed.

The finished product is a beauty.

The two new buildings.

That's it, folks!